I

FRANCIS

I

FRANCIS

LETTERS *to the* POPE
FROM AN UNLIKELY ADMIRER

DONNA SCHAPER

Fortress Press

Minneapolis

I ♥ Francis
Letters to the Pope from an Unlikely Admirer

Typesetting and interior design: PerfecType, Nashville, TN
Cover design: Brad Norr

Library of Congress Cataloging-in-Publication Data
Print ISBN: 978-1-5064-0861-3
eBook ISBN: 978-1-5064-0862-0

The paper used in this publication meets the minimum requirements of American National Standard for Information Sciences — Permanence of Paper for Printed Library Materials, ANSI Z329.48-1984.

Manufactured in Canada.

To the small group of women
with whom I read
Mary Daly's *Beyond God the Father*
over the course of one year.

Contents

Dear Francis, Will You Be My Boyfriend?

Dear Francis,

I shouldn't be having an affair with anybody, much less a pope. But if anybody can attract the attention of a sixty-nine-year-old happily married clergywoman, it's you. I've been looking for a spiritual leader like you my whole life, and looking in all the wrong places. I knew I was looking for a better father than the one I had, but I didn't know I was looking for a Papa. It turns out I was looking for someone like you, Francis. Until I met you, I had become slightly embarrassed to say I was a Christian, given what the punishmentalists were doing to give Christianity a bad name.*

I also serve a congregation in Greenwich Village in New York City where even the straight people like me are slightly queer. I've been ordained for decades, and I've been ministering here in New York for ten years. If you don't mind my saying, despite the unlikeliness of it all, I have fallen in love with you. I think you are the real thing. I don't think you're perfect, but I think I are damn good. You're probably as good as it gets.

I was born a Lutheran; a Missouri Synod Lutheran— that's the conservative kind. We Lutherans are known for our disdain of all things Catholic. We love to tell the story ad nauseam of our hero, Martin Luther, putting the Ninety-Five Theses up on your church's door. We love to tell how *your people* sold indulgences and *we* live by grace. We love to tell how *your people*

---

*By *punishmentalists*, I mean the people who imagine God is a judge rather than a gracious creator. I mean the people who are so pure that they only want to figure out who to blame. I mean the good/bad binary people, the ones on both right and left who find enemies and beat the crap out of them. I mean the ones so determined not to go to hell that they make hell, instead of heaven, on earth. God is grace and love and peace, not blame and shame. The blamers and shamers have punished themselves and God and given Christians a bad name.

let the pope tell them what to do and that's why *we* wouldn't think of voting for John Kennedy, a president who might follow a pope more than the Constitution. Today, Republican candidates for president who say that the Bible and their literalistic God is first place in their heart amuse me. That's the kind of slightly open-minded progressive I have become. I have a feeling we have in common the experience of religion-based opposition—for you, coming from the hidebound Vatican elite, and for me, from the hidebound evangelicals to my right.

Married to a Jew, with a daughter-in-law who's a rabbi—and three grandchildren who are learning Hebrew, one of whom who goes to Jewish parochial school—I have been pried open by difference and have learned to respect both Constitution and Christ. Uncanny, isn't it, that your theology resonates so powerfully with mine?

I know we're both trained as community organizers—me by Saul Alinsky and you by the streets of Argentina, brimming with liberation theology and more trouble than I ever saw. I know we are both sneakily political and really don't see the difference between politics and religion. I also know that we are bothered by the same things—the face of the poor and the desacralization of the earth—and that we have common enemies in instrumentalism (the way people use each other) and capitalism (that potentially good system that has gotten too big for its britches). I have very little of what Ross Douthat calls your "ostentatious humility." I am a woman. We can't afford to be meek.

But all excuses and differentiations aside, I shouldn't like you as much as I do. I used to hate your people with a vigor. I even wanted to title this book *Is the Pope Protestant?*, as a way of bringing you into my fold instead of my going toward yours. I wanted to use that old joke as a way of justifying how attracted I am to you. That way, I wouldn't be so embarrassed by my previously strong prejudices against your kind. I admit it: I am a recovering anti-Catholic bigot.

By the way, I'm not asking for forgiveness, which you have offered to other women who, like me, have had abortions. I do intend to repent of my bigotry, if not my abortion. One is sinful; the other is not.

My Missouri Synod Lutheran parochial school was next door to a Catholic parochial school. We hid in the bushes, laughing at the nuns, swearing to each other that they were so demented that they had pins stuck in their heads to keep their habits on. I used to cringe at the thought, in the way only a magical-thinking child can cringe at a presumed enemy who participates in her own bondage.

The only thing that tempered my family's prejudices against Catholics—the Polish ones and the Italian ones especially—was my mother's best friend, Helen. My mother never missed a chance to say that Helen had too many children. But they did talk on the phone every day, around ten thirty in the morning, and they loved each other. I often listened in on their conversations. My mother told Helen repeatedly to "use the pill," whatever that was.

You may as well know that I have picked a lot of fights with Catholics over the years—over abortion, over police brutality, over not being allowed to receive the Sacrament, over the way Catholics in the United States get to be political and no one notices that they're handing out voting cards during church. I really disagree with the Catholic Church about the meaning of religious freedom—yet that disagreement pales in comparison to what I see in you.

I wept the day Hurricane Sandy came through New York City. I went to check on our church building and realized the Catholics across the street were celebrating Mass. I could see through their window. The rest of the city was shut down, so I went to Mass. I prayed the prayers. I approached the altar to receive the wine and wafer. The priest took me aside and asked me if I was Catholic. He knew I lived across the street. I said no, I was not Catholic, and he refused to serve me. I flipped out, as much about the devastation of Sandy as the rejection implied in refusing me the Eucharist. When he wasn't looking, I stole a wafer. I also met with him for an hour afterward, and we fought and fought and fought. We became friends eventually. He never knew I had stolen the wafer. I didn't eat it. I just stole it. I'm admitting that to you now and asking your forgiveness. (I have often received the Mass at Chartres, just an FYI.)

I also jumped a liturgical fence at the installation of the Roman Catholic bishop in western Massachusetts. I'll tell you that story, too, after we know each other better.

I'll tell you what happened with the Lutherans and me. We broke up. When it became time for me to be ordained, I assumed I would become a Lutheran pastor. My heart broke when the Lutherans said no, even though they had paid for my seminary education. A fellowship from an organization called Lutheran Brotherhood even bought my books. It's a long story, told too often during these forty-four years of ordained ministry. For now, suffice it to say that I used to love the Lutherans. As one of the first women "ready" to be ordained a Lutheran, I was rejected once too often to hang around. For forty years last year, I have been ordained in the United Church of Christ, a much more open-minded denomination, which ordained the first woman in 1859 and the first gay man in 1960. As you will soon discover, I have a big bone to pick with you about women's and GLBTQ ordination. Maybe your pastoral ear will help you imagine why.

But Enough about Me

I first realized I was way too into you for normal feelings when I preached my first sermon about you. I had read the encyclical *Laudato Si* (meaning Praise Be) as soon as I began to hear the buzz. Everybody was talking about it and about you, and I am nothing if not a faddist. I love fads. And style. And buzz. You qualified on three levels. I figured you were an interesting fad. You had a cool car, a Fiat; you liked the spaghetti of the day and were putting on weight. You wore regular shoes.

You are not a fad, it turns out. You're going to last, even if something terrible happens to you tomorrow. (Yes, we worry about that. You are really out there. Maybe my letters to you will help protect you. And if they don't protect you from the demonic elements of both of our religions, at least the letters will let people know how important you are. They will show how you are not a fad but a man of faith.)

I didn't have any idea then how much competition I would have now in loving you. Not that I want you just for myself. I don't. But I was amazed by the way my pretty-obnoxious congregation received my sermons about you. I sort of whispered them at first. You know, trial balloons. Since irony always works in my pulpit, I asked sly questions, like this: "Wouldn't it be amazing if the pope became our environmental leader?" The response was overwhelming: people started smiling and clapping. And this is a tough, New York crowd!

Then when you said, "Who am I to judge?" regarding GLBTQ people, I flipped. I preached several sermons on that statement, thinking it a major breakthrough in just about everything, including the punishmentalist Christianity we both despise. I admit it: my theology is seriously reactive. I have been hurt way too many times by fundamentalist rigidity. I have seen Jesus abused so often—used as a hammer against gay people or divorced people or people who don't make a weekly mass or whatever it is that the punishmentalists think "those people" have done wrong—that I find it hard not to be reactive. Finally, I had something good to say about you and Jesus, all in the same breath. I was thrilled. And my congregation uncannily kept clapping. And clapping. And clapping some more. "Tell us more about the pope," they said in the narthex after the service.

We all knew you were coming to New York. I never thought I'd get to see you during your visit. I wasn't even the type of person who necessarily wanted to see you. But I surely never thought I'd get invited to see you. However, you know my friend Mary Sue very well. She was in charge of all the arrangements the cardinal made for your visit. You probably didn't know her partner, Nancy Jane. Anyway, you were very kind to both of them. They have something on their bureau you gave them. Who are you to judge?

Then, out of the late-summer blue, a letter from Cardinal Dolan came in the mail. The envelope came in the regular, boring mail. It looked much too fancy. The return address was Cardinal Dolan, Archdiocese of New York. I was afraid that it might resemble my last correspondence with the cardinal, which had not been pleasant. That was at the height of the Black Lives Matter trouble in New York. The cardinal had issued an op-ed in the *Daily News*, in which he argued that his constituents, the Irish cops, were not that bad. It was a sensible and sensitive defense. But it didn't go far enough, in my opinion, to articulate the daily devastations on the street where black people are so disrespected by violence and a culture of fear and harassment.

I published a different point of view, also in the *Daily News*, and the press had their fun watching a Protestant and a Catholic, a woman and a man, differ. I made sure I sent my dissent to the cardinal before I published it in the press. It was a matter of professional courtesy, and he sent me a letter thanking me for the heads-up. So I was familiar with the weight and look of the envelope. The envelope: heavy linen, embossed return address, a sense of the expensive. It was a very kind letter, thanking me for the courtesy of the heads-up. (Even though the cardinal doesn't use that kind of vernacular language, "heads-up," he does have the courtesy of thanking me for the courtesy.)

When an identical envelope appeared in my mailbox with a new message, that I was invited to meet *you* in New York, I was gobsmacked. I ran around showing the invitation to everyone, bragging insufferably that I was going to meet you. I was already making jokes all over town that I was in love with you and slyly tweaking you for being celibate while I was having an affair with you. The gender joking was and will remain important, I'm thinking, as our one-sided affair continues.

I even wrote a little story about my excitement, "What to Wear When Meeting the Pope." It made a big splash in my communities, most of whom had been as prepared as I was not to like you. I ending up wearing my clerical collar, of course, ordered from Clergy Couture, a European outfit that dresses ordained women with flair and fit. But, I wondered, should it be paired with a black skirt, the kind you wear to a foundation visit, or blue jeans, just to join your appreciation for those who work "in their quiet ways to sustain our life"? (I love the way you use simple language.) Or what about something with feminist flair, like my pink tights? Too hot for the situation and the season. The skirt won.

By the way, I rarely wonder about what to wear anymore. Wondering what to wear was a window on how important you had become to me. Before our affair, I didn't know how depressed I had been— spiritually, ecologically, and politically. You filled a void in my heart that I didn't really know was there. And you were so full of fullness! I'm almost embarrassed to say so. You are important in such an unassuming way that I doubt you care about how you look. You put the humble in the humility, the gravity in the gravitas.

You're going to put the word *pontification* out of business. You are refreshing religion. You have a bubbly joy in your escape from the security bubble. You are giving Christianity a good name. I never thought I would hear a congressional standing ovation for the Golden Rule, but now I have. Way to go!

Somehow it can't be accidental that the Harvest Moon rose the weekend you visited New York, or that the Muslim holiday Eid started the day before, or that the Jewish holy day Yom Kippur started that Tuesday evening. We were saturated with religion in New York City, with a great rising. And yes, alternate-side-of-the-street parking was suspended all week. Like my skirt, parking is a kind of sacramental preoccupation for those of us hungry for larger epiphanies. You are a large epiphany for me. You know the Latin, *epiphanos*—to be made manifest. I guess I'm really not that surprised about how much you mean to me. What is amazing is how you wowed all of New York City and manifested a glimpse of God to so many of us who had all but stopped looking.

The Day of Your Visit: September 26, 2015

Pope paraphernalia was everywhere for weeks before you arrived. We could buy a Pope Francis bobble head doll for $5.99 or a Pope Francis soap on a rope for $3.99. A special toaster from ToastThePope.com would imprint slices of toast with your likeness. An abundance of buttons, with slogans like "I ♥ Pope Francis," joined commemorative crucifixes on every street corner. Pretty much everybody in town was telling everyone else their religious history vis-à-vis Catholicism. "Who woulda thought?" was the main theme. For ex-Lutherans like me, the main theme was "Nobody hated the pope as much as I did." One cabbie asked me, "Who is the Pap? And why is everyone talking about him?" He was from Pakistan.

On the day of your arrival, even the police seemed to be smiling. There were traffic jams everywhere, and they managed the situation with smiles on their face. They were almost puffed up at the problem of attending to you. We were all basking in your sunshine. Martin Luther would have understood the vocation of managing sacred traffic. He was very fond of street sweepers, as you are. Right before the upcoming five hundredth anniversary of the Protestant Reformation in 2017, you were causing traffic jams in Manhattan. "Who woulda thought?"

You first refused to ride in your Bubble Car, then you rode it through Central Park. I appreciated your indecision. You were center stage long before you even arrived in the States, by way of Cuba no less. You seemed to like it there—Cuba and center stage. You even seemed to be having fun—although I wonder if one major event after another ever makes a seventy-eight-year-old like you tired. It appears not to. You went from one public appearance to the next, relaxed and always ready to shake another hand or bless another child.

Beyond dominating the media, you became the kind of uncanny celebrity whom people want to touch. My Baptist friend got to touch you, and he's still talking about it, as though the hem of your garment represented something akin to that of Jesus. I had a quarrel with him about precisely this: "Why did you jump over the fence at the prayer service at ground zero?! Since when are you, a Baptist, into touching 'his holiness'?" I want to talk to you about this hem business, seriously. I can't imagine that you believe in your own magic. (But if you do, that will probably help me fall out of love with you.)

At the National September 11 Memorial & Museum at ground zero, you wisely and strategically invited three hundred interfaith religious leaders to join three hundred "first responders," in one of those worship services that will mark the beginning of the next Reformation.

You inaugurated an interreligious age by inviting people to wear multiple garbs and gowns, chasubles and cassocks, brown-linen albs and African brocade, in the most religiously diverse city in the world, where even our public radio station uses the slogan, "Where eight million people live together in relative harmony." On September 26, 2015, we saw what this slogan means. It means color, if nothing else. The first responders wore their uniforms, and we wore ours. The visual contrast between the officers in blue and the clergy in stoles was intense. But there we were, side by side, uniformed on behalf of the largest possible security, listening to you speak of "peace." We were listening for the spiritual low hum, the same way the cops heard it in the traffic. We heard it, too.

You used the leader's power of invitation to bring people together. The people who assembled for the main service at ground zero are often warring and a threat to the public-radio promise of relative harmony. My hem-touching Baptist friend is a leader of Black Lives Matter. He speaks of war, not peace, with the police.

The year before your visit saw an ascendancy of quarrels between police and people, people often represented by those religious leaders sitting in the great museum. Many of us had been lying down in the streets chanting, "We can't breathe!" and "Black lives matter!" imitating the thirteen seconds it took Eric Garner to die while lying alone in the street. Police-community relations were in a period of serious strain. And yet there *we* were, and there *they* were, all dressed up with somewhere to go.

You brought us together. No one else could have.

You wisely chose to hold the prayer service in the Ground Zero Memorial's museum. It's in the basement, the undercroft, the bottom of where the twin towers used to be. It's decorated with the tortured metal beams from the ruined buildings, reminding us of the pride the towers used to command. Other unintended sculptures in the great hall, down deep in the city's most tragic cellar, include photographs of the dead being carried off, the police weeping openly. In one photo, the firefighters bring in Father Mychal Judge to say one more final rite. He died soon after. You mentioned him in your opening remarks. It was a brilliant inclusion in a place where people had been so flung apart.

Coming together with first responders involved the spirituality of shuddering and shivering. We were there where so many had died and so much of consequence to the last decade plus was born. We were there with those with whom we don't often agree. We were there because we had been invited—and because we had passed the four levels of security on the way in. I have never been groped so much in my life or passed through so many security monitors. Peaceful, I was not. Happy, I was.

I never got to see you up close. I wondered what the sea of cell phones looked like to you—and then I realized that's probably what all life looks like to you. I went back and forth about whether it was obnoxious to be in worship using one's cell phone. On the one hand, I wanted to argue for the momentousness of the moment, and I understand why people wanted to record it. It also felt overrecorded. There was a near humor to the sea of cell phones, almost as though we were more interested in Facebooking than in praying. We were wearing our vestments, bright, colorful, playful, unusual, packed together on small white chairs, where many of our robes intermingled with other robes. And we were all taking pictures of each other—but mostly trying, unsuccessfully, because of each other, to get your hem in view.

When you finally showed up, when we had been waiting the predicted hour, there was a great hush in the loud room, the one filled with ghosts and grief. Your simple gait as the guest of honor contrasted with what you could have been. You could have been the most pompous person in the room. People would have gladly carried you. There was a density to the moment, like the sacred density that was architecturally there. It went, as we say, viral. It occupied lots of space—and will continue to occupy lots of time. It was the end of an old kind of religion and the liturgical beginning of a new one. Appropriately, it was in a place drenched in death. You chose the place and the people. You wanted to cleanse it with the power of forgiveness and of Spirit. It wasn't exactly Easter, being September, but it was as close as my hem-touching friend and I are going to get.

I got a security headache just thinking about the event. You, the head of the world's 1.2 billion Catholics, led a multifaith prayer for world peace amid a somber moment of silence. That silence brought together Hindu, Buddhist, Sikh, Greek Orthodox, Muslim, and Jewish leaders. The place of death was packed with eager life.

"In this place of pain and remembrance, I am full of hope," you said. "I hope our presence here sends a powerful sign of our wish to share and reaffirm the wish to be forces of reconciliation, forces of peace, of justice." Religious leaders have heard and said these words so often that they are dusty within us. When you said them, you dusted them off.

In your one packed day in my hometown, from the United Nations to ground zero to church to Central

Park to Madison Square Garden, you brought the many different parts of New York City—including the ones that usually don't like each other—into something that felt strangely like unity. That feeling is strange, unusual, potent, and real.

New Yorkers are simultaneously remarkably secular and remarkably sentimental. We cry at the drop of a Broadway hat. But you with that simple gait had come to sing in a different key. We didn't think you had a price. You didn't seem to be afraid. You were different. "Start spreading the news, I am leaving today. . . . New York, New York. . . . If I can make it there, I'll make it anywhere." That's our local hymn, and it proved to be more than true of you. You even made New York look larger than it usually does—and yes, it often pretends to be larger and grander than it really is.

Did You Like the Prayer?

At ground zero, as you will recall, the substance of the event began with its astonishing opening prayer by Rabbi Eliot Cosgrove and Imam Khalid Latif. Every word in it matters and was attended. Remember: it took us three hours and four security checkpoints to get into the space. We weren't necessarily in the mood for a

long prayer. We were there for you, not for them. Then
they prayed so beautifully that we almost forgot about
you. You set a table for them. You didn't say much. You
didn't let the cardinal say much. You shared the liturgical space in a remarkable way, especially since it could
have been your show. It took much less time to get out,
yet no one really wanted to leave. After you left, people
just hung around.

Rabbi Cosgrove and Imam Latif, both exemplary
religious leaders in New York City, stood on the simple
platform to give this prayer as an opening to the liturgy.
It could have opened with prayer by a cardinal or a
monsignor or a priest or even a nun, but instead two
outsiders to the Roman Catholic Church inaugurated
the worship. That bringing in of the outsider is why we
pay attention to you. Rabbi Cosgrove began:

> In this place, where horrendous violence was com-
> mitted falsely in the name of God, we, the religious
> leadership of this great city of New York, gather as
> pastors to offer words of comfort and prayer. With
> love and affection, we recall the victims of the 9/11
> attacks. We pray that their souls, and the souls of
> those serving the FDNY, NYPD, PAPD, and NJPD
> are forever remembered for an eternal blessing.

Today and every day, may we understand our shared mission to be, in the words of Pope Francis, "a field hospital after battle"—to heal the wounds and warm the hearts of humanity in so desperate need of comfort.

Then came the imam, who happens to be a friend of mine. (My church is across the street from the NYU Catholic Center, where I stole the wafer, and the NYU Spiritual Life Center. Khalid and I are both chaplains there.) Khalid began this way:

Intolerance and ignorance fueled those who attacked this place. The courage of today's gathering distinguishes us from the opponents of religious freedom as we stand together as brothers and sisters to condemn their horrific acts of violence and honor each life that was lost unconditionally, as we read in the Qur'an that "one life lost is like all mankind" and "one life saved is like all mankind." To God all life is sacred and precious. Where others fail, let us be the peaceful reminders of that notion to His creation.

People often argue that Muslims don't condemn the violence that happened on September 11, 2001. Well, they did and they do. And Khalid did by your invitation! This power of invitation serves you well as a religious leader. I actually think of you as post-Catholic and post-Protestant. I think you're a religious leader who's not afraid of being a religious leader. You step out of your own corner, religiously, in order to open whole rooms of participation.

In addition to the mixture of secular security forces joining religious peace forces, and in addition to this profound prayer starting off what could have been a Catholic event, there was one more matter that permitted the spiritual density of the day. That was you setting a table. You had laid out a Mass without ever breaking a bread or tipping a wine. You were deeply sacramental without the sacraments. You were setting a new table, right here in New York City, at ground zero.

Enough about You and Me

I shouldn't have been so taken with you, but I was and am. I love what you have brought out in me—the way you have become my favorite spiritual antidepressant. I love you more than the wine I drink at the end of an evening or the wine that comes after we break our Protestant bread in our Protestant way. I love the way you managed Manhattan—gently, liturgically, appreciatively, uniquely. Most people like to "make it" here. You didn't seem to care about that. You have eased our spiritual constipation and made it safe to be a Christian again in the real world, even in New York City. I love the way you stick it to the phony Christians, of whom I hope I am not a member. OK, a little bit. Who am I to judge?

I love the way you set a table for me, and millions, to hear Khalid pray at ground zero. You came for peace, and you brought peace, a new peace, one that comes from the inside out.

I think you matter to a lot more people than me. I think you matter to us, as country and city folks, men and women, Muslim and Christian. I think you matter a lot. I already have it.

Love,
Donna

2

Dear Francis, What Are We Going to Do about the Poor?

Dear Francis,

I am so infatuated with you because you are going to change the conversation about poverty. Actually, you already have. Most of us ask the wrong question: "What are we going to do about the poor?" *Do* is the wrong verb. *We* may not exist. And there is no such thing as *the poor.* You are getting me out of my *doing* trap. You are dethroning me and liberating me at the same time. You are asking us to love the poor the way God loves the poor. You are asking us to stop fixing things. You are asking us to be different.

I don't know if I can. I'm not even sure you make it all the way to being different all the time. You, like me, often feel morally driven. And we both know that being morally driven is a kind of poverty, one that keeps us from the wealth of praise. Will your praise frame do anything to help the women who walk ten miles a day for water? I just can't stop trying to help—and I really want to help, and I'm not even sure *help* is the right verb. Your words have at least let me bang around in this cage with a little more vigor.

I'm on my fourth reading of the your encyclical *Laudato Si'* (Praise be to you), and the word *Praise* is the one that sticks with me. I pray it daily, hoping it will steep deep in me so that I can be liberated from the fix-it Protestantism that is killing others and me. I want regeneration, transformation, resilience, permaculture. I am desperate for them. I know I am damaged by my fix-it mentality because it's internalized capitalism. Internalized capitalism shouts, "You are in charge! Do something big and great, damn it. That's what God wants from you—to fix and control the earth." But I can't. I can't fix it.

Your words are profoundly different. You say the earth is already fixed. I so want to believe you. But I can't. I can't quite believe you. So much seems broken.

Why are so many people starving? When we get sick or injured, why do we think first about how much it's going to cost us? When did health care become a high-priced commodity? Why do some people live on $0.37 a day, and others on $37 a day? Why do New Yorkers allow Poland Spring water to be imported from Maine when we have great water here? So much seems broken.

I once got really depressed. For about six months, I wouldn't get off my couch. They called it Epstein-Barr virus or chronic fatigue syndrome. But I knew it was heartbreak.

I was a pastor in Riverhead, New York. One of the local nursing homes had twenty-four patients. I went to visit one of them, who was on my parish's membership list. Her diapers had not been changed for days. She was nearly comatose. I realized that the other twenty-three patients were in a similar condition: unattended, unfed, unwashed, left to sit in their own shit. Fix-it Protestant that I am, I went to work. I got the home closed down. There were press conferences and mighty talk about the depraved owners: "They only want to make money. They were paid by the state to house these people." The place opened up again in two months and became the same as it was before. I realized, over a long period of trying again, that there was not just one home like this. There were dozens. Certainly not all nursing homes or senior residences are this bad, but some are. And there is nothing you or I can do about it.

My learning was that there are Class A humans and Class B humans. There are the 99 percent and the 1 percent, and the 99 percent let the 1 percent control them/us. Black Lives Matter is a great slogan. It is not a reality.

My depression was both about the classification system that smelled right in front of me and about my own powerlessness to change it. I had love and ego twined around me. The depression eventually faded; I had three small children, after all. I went back to work but with my idealism packed away in an attic somewhere.

I have learned that most people don't need these dramatic experiences to become depressed about the poor and their own powerlessness about the poor. Most people already know there is nothing that can be done. That's why they say they hate politics or can't stand organized religion. They are pre-disappointed. They wear bulletproof vests against hope. They got the memo about money being everything. They know that people don't mean it when they say we should respect our elders.

They know. And I know. And I wonder if you know. I think you do. And I think what you know about pervasive poverty and the way many die in it, blaming themselves for it, is that we need to reframe the whole thing, not just our parts in it.

Blaming the poor for their poverty is directly related to the fix-it mentality. We could get fancy and call it the higher instrumentalism. When I give speeches about immigrants, I often put it this way:

> They pick our lettuce and strawberries, wash our dishes in fancy restaurants, and take care of our children and our seniors, all at a lower price than citizens born here are willing to accept. Then we tell them they are lawbreakers and deport them, as though the economy and environment in their own country hadn't already thrown them out. Blame and shame are the undercurrent of poverty. Those of us who think we care blame ourselves for not fixing it, while enjoying our strawberry shortcakes. Those whose money doesn't last the week or the month get blamed

and internalize that blame. It hurts. It is embarrassing
to be poor because "it must be your fault."

That's why I got irked with you in Paris at the 2015
Paris Climate Conference (COP21). Your opening
gambit was to beg the world not to commit suicide. I
understand what you were trying to say. But most of us
don't have the power to kill ourselves. We are getting
killed. As the Africans said, one day in Paris while walking out, "We will not die quietly."

You have given me a little hope that I might not
need to bang around in my fix-it/can't-fix-it cage forever. Thank you.

But still, do you know how bad it is?

The Encyclical's Big Ideas

I also pray the ideas in your encyclical as I try to steep
in them. Here I have italicized your words and kept
mine plain. Like me, you don't go for linear outlines so
much as circled and circling ideas.

*Integral Ecology. Culture, Nature, and economy are one breath
from a great God.* Look at you undermining capitalism and
undercutting the shallow environmentalism of people
who have gentrified the issue! If either poor or rich or

both believed the truth of this "one breath," all would be well. Bill McKibben said we didn't save the world at COP21, but instead we saved the *chance* to save the world. When the poor internalize their right to goodness and God, and the rich internalize their connection with the rest of the world, wow. Something could yet happen. I know *internalize* is a big word. What I mean is getting the goodness of the earth so deep inside us that we can't not praise. Thank you. I love so much of what you say, even the language you use to say it. You say:

We are not entitled to plunder. We have deified the market. The market is not God. Thank you for this revolutionary statement. So many of us think the market is God, and we bring it our offerings all day long, every day, even during our sleep. Thank you for starting a spiritual revolution against capitalism.

Our sister, Mother Earth. Protect our common home. Imagine that, our common home. The commonness of our home. The way we all belong and are all connected. If that were true, people wouldn't rot in their own diapers while being entrusted to people who weren't getting a decent wage.

Water is not for sale. The earth is our shared inheritance. Global inequality. You always say those last two together: *The earth is our shared inheritance, and still there is global inequality*. I have to know how you manage the glory and the treachery all at once. I mean, do you really know how much money ExxonMobil has? I wonder when your soul hurts at the disconnection between the truth of a shared inheritance and the way so many have stolen it from so many more.

How did somebody like you get to be pope in the first place? Didn't the authorities see you coming? As my friend, theologian Hal Taussig, puts it, you are so not cozy with empire. You are against empire. You see how awful it is that the poor populations will be most affected by climate change when they are the least responsible for it. How did you get to be so sincere when you say that the earth is our shared inheritance and that global inequality is wrong?

The crisis of anthropocentrism. Both you and I are in danger here. We so want to make a difference that we elevate ourselves to leadership when perhaps the butterflies should be in charge. Luther said we should sin boldly. I don't know how not to sin in self-importance when I think there might be something I could do about oppression of farmworkers, or at least increase respect for farmworkers. I want you to teach me.

Sacramental signs and the celebration of rest. Rest! What's that? I remember being in jail with Cesar Chavez and

Dorothy Day during the long farmworkers' strike in the 1980s. They were fighting for rest and money for the farmworkers. So, self-importantly, was I. I know you know something about the power of the deep rest of the sacraments that I don't know. I want that knowledge. I think the way you drive is a sacramental sign. Maybe that's why I jump liturgical fences as often as I can. I jump fences going to jail, and I jump fences to get to the sacramental rest. Somehow these actions and the desperate need for rest are sacramentally joined. I think you know how. I want to learn from you.

My favorite sentences from your encyclical follow here:

> "It is not enough, however, to think of different species merely as potential 'resources' to be exploited, while overlooking the fact that they have value in themselves" (par. 33).

> Creation has "an intrinsic value" that is "independent of [its] usefulness. Each organism, as a creature of God, is good and admirable in itself" (par. 140).

> "The Earth, our home, is beginning to look more and more like an immense pile of filth. In many parts of the planet, the elderly lament that once beautiful

landscapes are now covered with rubbish." I think you know why that resonates with me so.

"The idea of infinite or unlimited growth, which proves so attractive to economists, financiers and experts in technology . . . is based on the lie that there is an infinite supply of the earth's goods, and this leads to the planet being squeezed dry at every limit."

"The exploitation of the planet has already exceeded acceptable limits and we still have not solved the problem of poverty."

I love most the way you argue that the environmental and economic crises are primarily spiritual. I know: I have an implicit bias, having spent all these years in the church. But you say "spiritual" with authority, by not dividing the spiritual off into la-la land but directing it straight at the heart of human sin and human potential. Thank you, again. I am beginning to learn the meaning of integral ecology and our common home. You are taking me to the heart of what it means to be a human (par. 11). And I mean you are taking this human, Donna—not the other ones.

The Trouble

The first time I got in trouble for talking about capitalism was at my church in Miami. I was preaching a Christmas sermon and noted the word *taxed*. I said I would be glad to be taxed more if it would help the poor get out of poverty. A petition developed, and seventy-six of the twelve hundred members of my congregation signed it. One even interrupted my sermon three weeks later and said, "You can't talk politics from the pulpit." I found enough Spirit to walk down into the congregation, speak to him face-to-face, and suggest a conversation immediately after the service. Somehow I made it through the sermon while trembling inside. We had the conversation. I didn't get fired. I did get intimidated. I lost a bit of spunk over that.

I wonder how you challenge capitalism and so far seem to be getting away with it. I think it's because you challenge it so well. I keep wondering who your writers are. They have Jesuit clarity, Franciscan tenderness, and another quality that I can't quite name. It is a certainty, steeped in clarity and tenderness. It is often sneakily sly (I know I'm overusing that word and its friend *sneaky*).

You are sneaking up on us with forceful ideas, said so very quietly.

You don't seem to hate capitalism at all but instead love what might be there instead. You seem to believe in a universality of humanism, that all people really are human beings. You addressed the encyclical to *everyone*, which, if I didn't like you the way I do, I would call arrogant. You argue that people are not fundamentally greedy, an assertion that undercuts the narrative of capitalism at its knees. You think we need the awe and stillness of nature as much as we need things. You think we need to give and not just get. You think that the care of nature and the care of the poor are the same thing, and that we can't neglect either without losing the other. You don't think of the environment as something out there but as a whole, a big, bright package of goodness.

I wonder sometimes if your theory of evil is insufficiently well developed, and then I see the twinkle in your eye—the twinkle I want in my eye—and say I really don't care whether it is or isn't.

When you start from the premise of ecological wholeness and include humans and animals and stars and dirt all in one package, I get excited. I always start there and have spent my life resisting what my multiple degrees try to teach me, which is to separate, analyze, and critique. You launch an incredible attack on the appetites of capitalism and on the consumerist view of human nature. You make things whole that are flung apart. You have a different epistemology than that of critical realism. I like that, too. I'm not saying you're simple or unschooled. I'm saying you think very differently than the Enlightenment and its hegemonic control of the academy. You cohere rather than analyze.

You don't think there will be a technological or scientific fix, because the problem is a *moral* one and requires a moral and spiritual response. I sure hope you can sell that idea in the marketplace of ideas. (Yes, I'm being ironic.)

"How it clears the mind to have, at last, a pope who is unafraid," writes Gary Wills in the *New York Review of Books*. Of course, that lack of fear is what I like about you the most. If you're not afraid, why should we be? I, for one, am afraid for you. I think you're making the systems and their control freaks uncomfortable. I mean, I didn't even really challenge capitalism when I was arrested in Miami. I just got close to its front gate, and the guards jumped all over me.

For you, I'm afraid of the weight of the past and of the institution on your charisma. I've learned to be disappointed, and I am engaged in premature grief—it's

self-protection. I don't want my fragile hopes to sink
with yours. Adults get our hopes to the right size. We
"manage" our expectations, as if hope were a matter for
management. While I manage my hope and protect
myself from its grandeur, I realize that you have already
changed the conversation about poverty.

Now I want to know if we can actually change
poverty.

Unthinking the Way We Think about Poverty and Saving the Earth

Bill McKibben was right when he said COP21 in Paris
did not save the earth but instead saved the chance to
save the earth. He has also famously quipped that what
we did there might have been great if we had done the
same thing in 1995. When not frightened, I'm glad for
his measured hope. I agree with you that saving the
earth means saving the poor from the rich. I agree. And
I don't see the evidence yet for our shared hope.

I'm even cautious about the word *save*. We have to
figure out what it means to "save the earth." Surely, it
doesn't mean keeping the earth the same as it was in our
ideal year or was in our birth year or will be in our death
year. We environmentalists really have to watch that

language of saving, because it too often means pouring concrete over the present and hanging on for life to the way things never were. Things always change. They are always evolving. That's a good thing, not a bad thing. So first I quibble with McKibben's use of the word *save*. It's sneakily anti-Darwinian. You don't use it, but we both fall into a savior complex pretty quickly.

We may want to hang on to the earth we know but not the poverty that is its companion. I join you in liking good pasta. I join you in flying around the world a lot. I wonder if my appetite for feast is in my way. And I wonder if we are here to save the earth. Saving is so different from praising.

If saving means saving the natural evolutionary cycling of change without excessive human intervention, count me in. If it means some kind of keeping things the way they are right now, count me out. We who use so much water and so much fuel might have to use less of each. What would that mean for the poor?

I hate to bother you with my spiritual fears and my enjoyment of first-world status. Even being able to think about these matters as problems over which I might have some responsibility is problematic. I think you understand that. And thus you reframe the saving mentality as the praising mentality.

If praise means loving the earth so that you want its bounty spread around richly like peanut butter on a sandwich, count me in. If praise means safeguarding my bounty and my peanut butter, or even spreading less peanut butter on my sandwich, count me out. I won't find my way to praise without the joy and gladness being spread equally.

I have been reimagining the matter of saving and praising. See what you think.

I want to imagine the way we save the earth as more like a miracle. Not a deus ex machina kind of miracle, but instead a *deus en machina*, an awakenening in all of us. A miracle from within is the way composting and recycling have taken us over as normal practices. We aren't doing anything miraculous per se, but city streets now offer us a place to put reusable paper or cans. This large-scale change happened as miracle because we so wholly participated in recycling on smaller scales. Naomi Klein puts it well: "Everything must change," and that means every*one* must change. In her book, *This Changes Everything*, she is telling us that it is not just that we drive or the way we drive but also the way we eat and think and pray. Large change is required; small change is all we know how to do. Must we have less so others have more? And is there really enough for everyone?

Doesn't overpopulation bother you as much as people using contraception? Does your heart not hurt about there being so many of us? What does hurt your hearrt, you who want to join me in changing everything and not knowing how to start?

Einstein said there are two kinds of people: those who think there are two kinds of people and those who don't. Just kidding. He allegedly said the two kinds of people are those who don't believe in miracles and those who think everything is a miracle. I am part of the latter tribe. Sometimes I can't believe I can talk to a friend in Australia and get a response in real time. Skype is a miracle. Plus it doesn't cost an arm and a leg. Other times, I marvel at the High Line, an old rail line converted into a garden walk in New York City, and how smart the tourist industry is, even in the way it overpopulates the High Line. Or I think about that rare painted bunting that showed up in Brooklyn looking for a good cup of coffee. Or at least I think that is why a tropical bird showed up in Brooklyn. I can't think of another good reason. I panic at the sheer thought of managing or organizing an equal distribution of birds or beauty or technology. Somehow you don't seem to share my panic. Maybe that is the source of my simultaneous fear and love of you.

Definition of a Miracle

I hope you don't mind a little Bible study. Jesus turned water into wine. He turned a social nightmare into a social dream. He concentrated his power and turned scarcity into feast. He did what his mother told him to do. Is it just my fantasy, or did Jesus have a mind free of fear? Was he trying to define a miracle for us? I'm not sure. He may just have been showing off. But he helped me inch toward a definition of a miracle: it's something for which we don't have to pay. Miracles give us things beyond the reach of our payments. They are acts of grace for which we don't have to work. They involve our turning a corner, reversing field, tilting our mind's head in a different direction—returning home by a different path, as Joseph wisely did to protect that baby Jesus.

Money is a metaphor for many things. It's not just the capacity to buy peanut butter or telephones or fossil fuels. It is the coin of exchange. There are many kinds of exchanges, and often I think I love my status even more than I love my things. I am on the "top," and from the top, we can safely worry about poverty.

Sometimes we work for money so people will think we're good. Or we work so people will think we're right. Or we work for money because money rules us. Being good, being right, and getting money are basically the traffic jams in our brains. They clog our minds. They are fearful congestions.

Our motivations are rarely to prepare for the concentration of grace because we're so busy preparing for the concentration of works. As James Forbes often preached, "Somebody done turned the wine into water." We live in the opposite of the miracle of grace. Being good, being right, getting money, avoiding shame or blame—these are our major activities. They keep us in the traffic jams of fear, and we are congested by these fears. We hardly have the freedom to move or turn a corner or look at things from the point of view of praise.

The rate of miracles (payment-free activities) has been decreasing as the rate of commodification has increased. Praise goes to the wayside as accumulation takes its place, and the very accumulation that destroys the earth also creates fear. I may be rich, but I'm also scared of not being rich. You are status-rich and could have all the money or luxury or things you want. You refrain from wanting them in order to make room for praise. I like that a lot about you.

It turns out that even this late in the history of Christendom, most of us are spiritually dumb, even idiotic or moronic. We say we don't believe in miracles, meaning we don't believe in what we are given. Instead we believe in what we can get. By sin, I mean the avoidance of the miracle of grace.

How did you get to be different? What flipped your spiritual switch so that you could be spiritually smart as opposed to spiritually stupid and captive? How did you learn how to praise instead of grab? How did you learn not to be afraid of losing the crutches that I seem to require?

I think of myself as spiritually handicapped or spiritually retarded, not spiritually well or spiritually smart. When we can't fathom a miracle, or something for which we need not pay or earn, we are spiritually handicapped. We resist the very thought—the thought of grace and miracle—that could save our evolutionary cycle and consequently stop grinding the face of the poor.

They say more than half of Icelanders believe in elves and trolls. We probably find that charming or in some other way condescend to the people who know only what they can see. Something about our first-world education stole magic and mystery and miracles from us. I'm trying to figure out why they weren't stolen from you and why you remain free for praise. I have hope that when I figure this out about you, I'll find the way to praise.

For everything to change, we need a miracle. We need the miracle of the uncongested mind, the one that can concentrate on grace and not works, the one that can be ready to receive that which can't be bought. Then we can "go to work" on "saving" the environment while not destroying it by the sly fantasy that we are the ones saving it.

I guess you are pastorally astute enough to know the real source of that depression I had long ago. I think of myself as a Class A human and don't want to become a Class B human. Thus my crutches and my distance from the praise you and your patron saint propose. I'll keep talking if you'll keep listening. Suffice it to say for now that I am scared to be as good as you. I'll just have to stick with loving you while trying to learn how to believe in miracles.

Love,
Donna

3

Dear Francis, Missed You in Paris

Dear Francis,

You may or may not know it, but you rocked the 2015 Climate Conference (COP21) in Paris—the twenty-first Conference of the Parties, where delegates from 192 countries worked together to fashion a new international agreement on climate change. I couldn't believe my ears or eyes as one world leader after another quoted you. Over and over again, they declared, "This is a moral issue, involving both the economy and the environment simultaneously." You did what Occupy Wall Street did in New York: your encyclical changed the language about class to income inequality, and on top of that, you framed that issue within an environmental and systemic economic crisis. And you weren't even there in person! I was so proud of you—and proud of me for having fallen in love with you. I pick well.

Of course, I had to figure out how to get to Paris for COP21. It was the place to be for those, like me, who feel threatened to our cores by climate change and have become hopeful about your leadership. I wanted to watch how your words would reframe the conversation. You prevailed by framing the language of the conference: no one dared talk about two degrees Celsius, which had been the proposed ceiling on the amount of warming to be accepted. Instead, the speakers declared climate change a moral problem. By moral, they meant something we do for others, especially our grandchildren and especially the global south and low-lying areas. By moral, they meant the Golden Rule with its particular emphasis on the suffering neighbor. By moral, they used your terms linking ecology and the environment. And you weren't even there! But still your encyclical framed the conference, especially its results.

You mattered. I like to join praise to impact, spirituality to effectiveness, and you're doing that.

I don't need to teach you what a frame is. You already know that a frame is what makes a picture, choosing to leave some things in and leave others out. For me, it's a powerful form of leadership. We pastors and priests—medics in your field hospital—use frames all the time. We use them in counseling situations where people say they don't know how they will go on after a loved one dies. Instead, we often say, the time will come when you will no longer see your life in the frame of your loved one being gone. You won't know when that time will come before it comes but you will wake up one morning and realize you are in a new frame. We use them politically to talk about homelessness or the murders of young black men on the streets of American cities. We say there is a deep and pervasive inequality and we know it is wrong. We tell one sad story after another. We frame these issues morally all the time, but very few people listen. Most people think the moral frame is pie in the sky.

You brought the pie to the skies—and the world's leaders. From their mouths issued the frame that climate change is a moral issue. The other possible frames for COP21 were political or scientific. Each of those would have left out the spiritual and moral. Many people in power like to do that. Your frame kept in these perspectives, making a more beautiful, human, historical, and natural picture. It was what you repeatedly call ecological integrity in process. It is not a direct quote. It is what we need.

Getting the nations to an agreement at COP21 was a long journey, starting with the United Nations Framework Convention on Climate Change, adopted in Rio de Janeiro in 1992, acknowledging the existence of anthropogenic (human-induced) climate change as a major threat to a sustainable planet. The first climate treaty to emerge from this process was the Kyoto Protocol, which commits industrialized countries to internationally binding emission-reduction targets. It was passed in December 1997 at COP3 in Kyoto, Japan, and finally came into force in February 2005, when a sufficient number of developed countries had signed the agreement. The United States did not sign, hampering negotiations for the next decade. Why didn't the political and scientific frame prevail? Probably the reason was the lack of someone like you to provide religious and moral leadership. I can't guarantee that, but I know your reframing made a difference this time, at the twenty-first conference.

COP21 reminded me of every United Church of Christ General Synod I have ever attended: all the action is on the border between the inside and the outside. Huge pavilions of hangers-on, like me, stood next to the ministers and the delegates, the insiders who would make decisions. We hung in and hung on. And we needed language that was powerful.

At first, I thought we would probably save the rich and not the poor, the centers but not the peripheries, the north and not the south. Forgive me, Father, for I have sinned. I don't have the hope you have. You are and were the wild card. And you even had more power than we needed. The Vatican website had 3.4 million hits on your speech to the insiders at the United Nations, which came on the first day. Then you left, kenotically. You suggested what's obvious to the outsiders: let's not commit global suicide. I am still quarreling with your suicide frame, for I don't think powerless people have enough power to commit suicide. I think they get killed. The metaphor could have been homicide, not suicide. But I do know what you mean: Let's not participate in our own demise, even if we have a well-protected cynicism.

As New Jersey's governor Chris Christie likes to argue, "We've always had climate change." Yup, and we have always had poverty, and we have always had disproportionate impacts from what Oxfam calls "extreme carbon emission inequality." But we've never had climate change that threatened to put so many low lying lands under water. You know how serious the problem is and bring us to its severity with hope in your heart. I appreciate that!

Because of you and a thousand actions that surrounded your spiritual leadership, the conference was a political and moral success. I was so glad that the entry that won the World Wildlife Federation poster contest was the knockoff of the Delacroix painting about the French Revolution, "Liberty Leading the People," and was papered all over the RER, the regional train system that runs out to the conference center. Replacing Lady Liberty in the poster is a panda holding the WWF flag as a sign of resistance and hope; following close behind Lady Panda is a young woman waving a poster in one hand and toting her skateboard in the other. These prize winning posters from a contest done by the World Wildlife Federation appeared in many Metro stops and were reproduced in dozens of ways by ordinary participants. The poster illustrates the same fierceness the French showed on the Sunday two weeks before the conference's start, when the police canceled the giant kickoff march in response to acts of terrorism. Barred from demonstrating in person, protesters laid their shoes in rows on the street; they amused themselves and many others with the *amuse-bouche* of the human spirit. The question was the spirit of the world leaders who imagine themselves the main course. Bill McKibben rightly said that success, measured as setting the goal for allowable warming below two degrees, would have been a good result in 1995. But Francis, we didn't have a pope like you in 1995.

We didn't have a pope—or frankly, any spiritual leader—before now. Now you are here, and you really matter. You know enough of the science to understand resilience. Your encyclical parallels the secular ideas of resilience and permaculture. It is not anti-scientific so much as scientific-plus. The permaculture periphery is where hybridity and excitement happens; it's where we are suspicious of any of the insiders who imagine they are the human center, which they are not. Humans are part of the world, not the whole world. We might even be closer to the periphery or the edge of the universe than we think. In permaculture we love the way we are part of the whole. In resilience we imagine ourselves as part of evolution, not as guiding it.

Just as permaculture encourages the participation and resilience of all the parts of nature, you were using religious language to encourage the participation and resilience of earth-loving women we see on posters riding skateboards. The young woman and the other followers of Lady Panda in that poster were the main clients for the COP21. Everybody wanted to uphold that skateboard bearer and her idealism. You did by your frame. She did with her picture and all it evoked to the human evolutionary project.

I'm not going all the way to hope; the conference implementation has just started. I do hope in the skateboarder and the pope. But I'm feeling resilient, which is different from hopeful. Those inside the ecological integrity of the permaculture, those who know resilience, are surely our friends. And you have befriended them.

The Obstacles to Hope

The threat of terrorism was never far away in Paris. My Francophile, French-speaking husband, Warren, came with me. We had our honeymoon in Paris, know the city well, and have been there at least once a year for nearly forty years. Warren insisted that we go directly to the square known as the Place de la République, where mourners had flocked following terrorist attacks in January and again in November 2015, just three weeks prior to COP21. I didn't want to go see the evidence of terrorism as I was fixated on finding my lost hope. I knew that terrorism has a chance of dismantling your frame. It still does. But Warren was right: I needed to see the shoes. I also needed to see the protests in the streets that happened anyway. Believe me, I know that this whole matter of potentially devastating climate change is not all about my hope or me. I also know that my precarious hope is the spiritual situation for millions. We need help with our hope. You help.

Day two for Warren and me (day five for the COP21) found us involved with a man high up on a light pole, waving a homemade banner of the earth with a fetus wombed in it. He was in front of the Grand Palais, an enormous glass-roofed building constructed for the 1900 Paris Universal Exhibition, where we were trying to see opening day of an exhibit called Solutions COP21. That was a mistake! You'd think New Yorkers would know how to get tickets. We found ourselves standing outside, oddly displaced, even though we were already siding with the outsiders. The man on the light pole in his ruggedness and raggedness—the flag had seen more than one demonstration—paled next to the size and elegance of the building. The young man on the pole was held up by the agility that had propelled

him high above the hundred-plus cops staring at him
with machine guns in their hands.

COP21 was never far away from terrorism. If anything, the timing of the Paris terrorism and another
attack in San Bernardino halved much of the press
coverage that the convention's great story might have
received. Further, demonstrations were verboten. How
were we going to get the street power we needed to
hold politicians and planners accountable if we couldn't
go into the streets? That was a big question in Paris,
almost as big as the one you made us face about what
moral is and is not.

But the demonstrator in front of the Grand Palais that day was held up not only by his own physical
strength, but also by the energy of fifty or so protesters,
meekly shouting their support. A dozen police trucks,
ready to arrest him and the demonstrators once their
hero came down, backed up the gendarmes. Due to the
state of emergency in the city, the police weren't kidding. On the other side of the Grand Palais was a long
line of people, maybe two hundred, waiting to get into
the major exhibit of the moment ("Objective: provide
a large target audience with an overview of the many
products, services, processes, and innovations either
existing or under development throughout the world

to fight climate change and its impact"). That line had come to a full stop, even though it was the line for people with reservations. We had gone for the show, not the protest.

Being the kind of people who can neither climb poles nor stand in long lines nor wait to get busted by the French riot police, we went across the street to the Petit Palais. There we enjoyed a wonderfully quirky permanent collection (featuring some amazing Courbet nudes) and a striking courtyard garden. From our perch in the Petit Palais, we watched the bookended scene. Demonstrators to the right, police everywhere in the middle, and technology nerds to the left. In the time it had taken us to enjoy the exhibit, the pent-up energy of the waiting crowd and the pent-up energy of the protesting crowd had diminished, leaving us with a pent-up set of questions.

The illegal sit-ins and pole climbings and ethical spectacles were everywhere. They were imaginative and fierce—insisting that the global climate emergency needs to trump France's state of emergency. Naomi Klein (in agreement with your ecological integrity) was arguing that people had to reclaim the streets on Saturday, no matter what the agreement was or wasn't. We humans have a real interest in our liberty. The prohibition against protest was central to the conference's muting—and the word still got out, but nowhere near as forcefully as it might have without the terrorist attack and its shut-downs. One group got into the Louvre and poured oil on its floors. Why? To punctuate the way oil companies, like the French Total company, had insinuated themselves into all the aspects of our lives. Why? "For *liberté, égalité, fraternité.*"

I remained deep in questions. How will the world find a way to express itself if the streets are closed by one measly piece of terrorism after another? Where will all the energy go? If we can't use the streets, we may more than ever be reliant on encyclicals and spiritual leadership and hits on blog posts.

You, Francis, are like the pent-up energy of solar and wind—energy bottled up because interests rise up against its use. Spiritual power also is too often pent-up because of the failure of religious leaders—your people and my people and other religious people. We have failed to gather spiritual energy. We have driven people away from spiritual energy. While certain people worry that some coal and oil will be "stranded assets," meaning the coal will be left in the ground or some gasoline won't go into a car's tank if we alter the direction of energy use, my question is how to release the pent-up spiritual energy, so that we can hope enough to do enough to help ourselves.

Maybe if I had gotten into the exhibit, I would know more about these rival energy sources. Or if I had braved the demonstration, I would know more about that energy—the kind that lets people un-pent, even re-pent. But both absences drove me more clearly to your spiritual energy, stranded as it is. You might argue that "pent" spiritual energy is our main resource. And actually, it is easy to obtain and resilient enough to regenerate itself. That is what I was learning from you, even as I was stranded between art and politics on the streets of Paris.

The Serenity Prayer in Paris

I did more praying in Paris than I usually do. Mid-conference, I realized I was half hopeful, which was better than 5 percent hopeful—and that also I was scared of hope. I remembered the world-famous "Serenity Prayer": *God, grant me serenity to accept the things I cannot change, courage to change the things I can, and wisdom to know the difference.* It is most helpful to addicts and is used widely by people in Alcoholics Anonymous. Since many of us confess we are addicted to fossil fuels and will use some to go to work today or cook our food today or warm our homes today, it seemed like a good prayer to pray. Like that drink you can't stop drinking, we are stuck in an addictive pattern. We are morally compromised, to put it mildly. And we believe—don't *know*, but *believe*—we have the spiritual energy to break out, even if all the systems of our lives are set up against the breakout.

I was powerfully reminded of the United Church of Christ Synod last July in Cleveland, where a caucus of us proposed a Stop Fracking resolution. We spent hours on national phone calls debating when fracking should be stopped. We finally proposed 2030 as the last fracking date. It was compromises after many "brackets"—what COP21 calls the matters that are kept in parking lot, where we put the things we don't know how to decide. The synod amended our so-called radical proposal and unanimously passed 2017 as the final date. We were gobsmacked, bemused, amused by the fact that our people were more ready to go cold turkey than we were.

Something like that was happening around COP21. The people who know what it will take to do anything, much less something, much less something serious about rising sea levels, are trying to accept serenity. The people who are fed up and on the outside are much more ready to get serious. They, like the people inside, have grandchildren. But the outsiders know what it means to get screwed. The insiders don't. Forgive the inelegant language, Francis, but I think you get my drift. If you and I are to be friends, you're going to have to learn to put up with a little (maybe a lot) of irreverence.

Once you've said yes to a moral frame, the questions come rolling in like a tsunami. Most have to do with what the first-world polluters will pay in repentance and compensation for warming the planet. Other questions have to do with gender equality and refugee status. Why omit these matters? Because there remains a fantasy among the insiders that we can deal with climate without dealing with it justly. We may need more than the tragedy of terrorism to wake us up.

The translation of Jesus' frequent words about the poor is not just the word *poor*. It should be translated "the oppressed poor." It matters that we get the relationship between the rich and the poor right. I am having my affair with you because you get it. Many, many otherwise decent people don't.

Back to the Serenity Prayer. Most people among the privileged class focus on the *accepting* part. They have the patience to be patient. The prayer is actually more balanced. It could also be called the Change Prayer. It could also be called the Wisdom Prayer. Again, forgive me, Father, for I have sinned. There is no they. There is only a we. And surely I am part of the privileged we and the underprivileged we: both/and, not either/or.

Maybe you and I could go out to dinner with Al Gore, the consummate pragmatist. You argue against instrumentalism, the way we use things that we should instead love. Gore is a brilliant instrumentalist and politician. Gore asks the moral questions this way: What must we do? What can we do? What will we do? His triplet joins the triplet of the prayer. Of course we will have to accept some things that won't budge. Of course we have to change what we can. And mostly we need the wisdom to know the difference. That wisdom will come from looking at the climate from the bottom up, not from the top down. That wisdom will come from spiritual energy—since we can no longer fossilize ourselves.

Listen to my friend the business-environment journalist Marc Gunther express his dismay in the blog on his website. By the way, he also likes you a lot. He is another one of us who has "hope in the pope." Marc is also the godfather of my son—the one with the three grandchildren. They are like my clients as I write and struggle morally for wisdom. I write for them and the world they will inherit. Here's what Marc posted on December 9, 2015:

> I wish I could be optimistic about COP21, the cli-
> mate negotiations coming to an end in Paris. I can't.
> Even if the world's countries keep their promises—
> known, in the mind-numbing argot of the UN as
> Intended Nationally Determined Commitments—
> the climate reductions they are promising don't go
> far enough. . . . These unenforceable "commitments"
> are, at best, a step in the right direction and, at
> wors[t], a way for government leaders to try to fool
> their citizens and, perhaps, themselves into thinking
> they are doing the right thing. (marcgunther.com)

Despair will join terrorism in promoting our fears—those that we use to protect ourselves from hoping. If self-protection flourishes, the earth will be in even more peril than it already is. How do we get to the politicians who will actually make the decisions that you and I want them to make? How do we get even more influence for what the world's majority of people want to do, for what creation intended, and for what would actually constitute praise? I think it has to be spiritually solar, deep grailing (like the holy grail that many assume is the blood and trail of Jesus in the deep underground). Instead of fracking and hammering at what is deep underground, we need to flow *with* it, from under the ground, as renewable as energy itself. That kind of energy has the capacity to overcome the obstacles—those inside those and us all around us.

My Religious Experience in Paris

I would never have found the Jesuit Church of Saint Ignacio in the sixth arrondissement if I hadn't snuck into the high-end department store Bon Marché, the neighbor that dwarfs the church, early on a Saturday. I knew about taking care of my spirit while at a large international conference in a large city, especially a conference preoccupied with talking about the end of the world as we know it. The Bon Marché was minutes from the apartment we had rented for the duration of my focus on the end times. (The apartment was splendid: built in the sixteenth century, small, efficient, with automatic lights that turn on when you ascend to the second *étage* or second floor.) The Bon Marché was garbed in purple light, wrapped in red Christmas ribbon, giving the word gaudy new meaning. With the heightened security in Paris, the swanky department store was seriously protected by smiling guards who requested a peek into every purse.

After my walk through Bon Marché and a few squirts of free Chanel No. 5, I strolled north a block and saw the sign. Modest, without either purple or much of any other hue of light, the permanent sign said, "Eglise Saint-Ignace." The less-permanent sign said, "Taizé Service Saturday night, 5 December, 20:30." My heart jumped for joy. No train to take. No plane to make. No more security checkpoints to pass. Convenience was as high as spirituality on my mind. The church, though likely to be crowded later at the Saturday-night service to pray for you and the climate conference, didn't want to peek into my purse. It wanted to peek into my soul and would be willing to give me a free seat in exchange.

I popped quickly into the church to check it out. It is compulsory to walk in and out of a lot of churches when you are in Europe, part of the overall self-improvement we Americans feel when abroad. To my right was a half-life-size crèche with African shepherds and Wise Men—those first scientists—an African baby Jesus, and some sheep with very long legs. As someone who collects crèches from different nations, in hopes that Jesus will prevail artistically if not theologically, I counted my trip already consummated.

Imagine my surprise when going in further to the
large Gothic nave, I discovered it empty, even though
it was hours before the service. The interior had been
rearranged into a wide elliptical space. The moquette
carpet on the floor was clean, making a place suitable
for sitting. The wooden cross was portable, and I could
tell it had been moved around a lot. I have always liked
Jesuits and Saint Ignacius (1491–1556), the Catholic
saint who knew how to question empire intelligently. In
fact, I have often thought that if I wanted to spend the
rest of my life convincing Catholics to ordain women,
I'd start with the Jesuits and apply for status with them
myself. Why? Because they are smart enough and stra-
tegic enough to still question empire.

I had wanted to spend the weekend praying for the
conference anyway. Enough policies, enough words,
enough politics. All the ministers were off till Monday,
or so they said. It was time for me to pray. My spirit
needed more than its usual security system, something
larger than its usual guards. Plus, I had looked up the
parish online and knew that I, as a consumer of religious
services, would be pleased with this service; Jean-Marc
Furnon, who was chaplain there from 1999 to 2007,
had instituted a long time of silence and lectio divina,
in a Mass that drew youthful participation.

We arrived a little late on Saturday night, for reasons that you can blame on Bill McKibben. We had gone east to a Paris suburb called Montreuil, where there was supposed to be a mock trial of ExxonMobil. We couldn't find it but instead found the entire people's alternative conference to COP21 and had way too much fun to get back to church on time.

When we finally arrived at the church, it was standing room only. Hundreds of young people, the kind that can cross their legs and sit for a long time on the ground, were snuggled together on the rug. The half dozen or so Jesuits in white robes were kneeling, again with a flexibility that was more than just spiritually impressive. The candles were lit. The contralto joined the tenor, who joined the guitar, backed up by the violin, in "Laudate Dominum." That was followed by "Alleluia 20," then "Bless the Lord," then the "Kyrie 18." We got two of the last seats. When we started my favorite Taizé song, "Jesus, Remember Me," I had my first good cry for the planet, the people, you, and me. "Ubi caritas" and "Misericordias Domini" and "Nada te turbe" closed us out.

Most important was the motion of the cross. Four strong young ones—the demographic of COP21—picked up the cross, turned it upside down, and turned it into a table, which they then knelt before and kissed. Then the robed Jesuits did the same. Then people from all four corners of the earth, I mean the chapel, stood quietly and slowly and did the same. Then I did the same. My Jewish husband held my coat. He had never been to a Taizé service and spent most of it spiritually overwhelmed. Then from the north, the south, the east, and the west of the sanctuary, people lined up to do the same. No bread, no wine, only a cross to kiss. I was so glad to be worshipping without having to jump some silly fence.

You were adequately prayed for. The planet will be all right. *Nada te turbe.* (Let nothing disturb you.) Worship and praise, song and light, crosses carried—these are the renewed and renewable meanings in me, most of the time. That night, they were more than renewed. They were realized.

Ethical Spectacle and That Pesky Climate Ribbon

While at the alternative people's conference, we had run into the climate ribbon, which was as liturgical as the Taizé version of the Mass. On the Climate Ribbon Tree, people write down in one sentence what they fear to lose. They say things like waterfalls, or clean, breathable air, or food, or hope. The ribbon is a powerful visual, a cultural tree of confession and lament. People get "out" what is worrying them. They carry their confession around in a unification of their message.

Andrew Boyd, my friend from New York, helped create the climate ribbon. (We had also helped create the Wall Street Bull used for Occupy in New York City.) Andrew and I had to have "words," friend to friend, in a suburb of Paris.

My church, Judson Memorial in New York City, was the first site for the climate ribbon, which by now had gone worldwide. We had also managed to lose three thousand of the original ribbons. Someone threw them out at my over-busy church. Andrew was not happy. Neither was I. We were both a little exhausted that winter afternoon. We came to an understanding and laughed at how important mistakes were going to be, going forward in this large task of reducing temperatures. We also came to understand forgiveness.

Mid-conference on that weekend, we were both tired and afraid. We knew you had prevailed in setting the moral tone and that things were looking "abnormally" good. We knew you had made for hope large enough for the world, good enough for the globe, challenging enough for the cosmos. And there we were, writing our hopes and fears on small, flimsy ribbons, some of which we had already lost, as though they really weren't important at all. We were forgiving each other for small stuff like losing some of the people who wanted a voice in the matter. But at least we were writing our fears and our hopes on the ribbons. Some would be lost. Some not.

Oddly, this time with my agnostic Jewish friend Andrew was my confession on the way to the Taizé service. We knew we were very, very small in that moment together.

The Big Surprise of Paris Was How Spiritual It Was

I figured I would have a spiritual experience in Paris. I always do—sometimes just around the celeriac or carrot salad or the geraniums in the windows. But I was surprised that the world was having one. And it was. It was because of you. Your blessing was palpable. Whether the words were resiliency or hope, fear or serenity or forgiveness, or ethical spectacles—or people kneeling before crosses instead of skateboarding—our kinds of spiritual words dominated the language and the event.

Even that wonderful number, two degrees Celsius, took a backseat to the matter of renewing our spiritual energies. And that we did do in Paris, thanks to your encyclical and its jump start. You got followers—which is the main way to tell if someone is a leader. Leaders have followers. You are a leader.

Love,
Donna

4

Dear Francis, We've Got to Talk about Women

Dear Francis,

Warren and I had a great time at the climate conference. He knew how much I was thinking of you. We have few secrets after 34 years together. But then we had to go back to the new normal—where terrorism will vie with renewables at every moment, for both press attention and actual money. We had to go home and remember that women are still second-class citizens in the Catholic Church. We had to realize that you and I orbit different planets—you at home in Rome, me at home in New York, still feeling like one of those strange women who have "Rev." or "Mother" in front of our regular name, still remembering that you and I both love Jesus and serve him sacramentally. On Sunday you and I both broke the bread and poured the wine. We both said a prayer begging the Holy Spirit to enter the elements and enliven them with memory of Jesus. Then we parted ways—and not just because we are in different time zones. We are in different worlds, too, plugging along together and also not really together.

You have good reasons for being opposed to women's ordination. Your institution has never done it before. You love your church. How could you be pope and not love it? You have already challenged the market economy, which is twice as prophetic a behavior as challenging the presumably internal issue of women's ordination. The problem we share with capitalism may get you killed—or as you know, that's what lots of people say. It won't get me killed, because I have a congregation and denomination that agree with me about its peril. You may not get away with a challenge to capitalism. And you might not get away with challenging your system about women, but I think you could go a lot further with it than you imagine.

How can I be an admirer of your larger project—slyly and spiritually saving the environment and the economy as two sides of the same coin—and ask you to do more? I should have said in that last letter that the root of the word *save* or *salvation* is *shalom* or *security*. But I'm not going to repeat myself. Here I have big fish to fry, and I'm going to fry them with all I've got.

I'm going to tell you why I think you *have to* move on women's ordination. Your whole project is in great peril if you reject my plea. It's not just a personal plea, but it certainly starts there. It's a plea for your whole project.

The first reason is that you will actually prejudice the sincerity of your project if you don't ordain women. That project puts praise over use by brilliantly telling us that we have to move beyond the concept of "versus" altogether. We have to live in one whole world, one whole universe, where we don't have second-class anythings.

You won't be able to do that without ordaining women. Or without including the other at all levels of every project. It is simply too glaring and glib an omission. You can't refuse the other-ing of animals and species and forget about women.

I am convinced that if we could just sit down and talk through the ordination of women and GLBTQ people in the Catholic Church, we could come to an understanding. Your own inner logic of inclusivity would lead you to conclude that healthy religion doesn't exclude half of the population from full, clerical participation. Your own inner spiritual logic about animals would require you to address the question of women's role and participation in the world. Why does the *Laudato Si'* encyclical talk more about species diversity than it does about gender inclusivity? Don't the two parallel each other as spiritual forms of inclusion, which unthrones the "man," the one who falsely thinks he is in charge of earth, land, sea, and females? You couldn't possibly want to allow internal institutional matters to topple your project. It's too important, and you know it.

The second reason I want to talk about gender inclusivity, at all levels of church and world, is that it's the right thing to do. Right now, you will hold your followers, the spiritual-but-not-religious people, and the "none of the above" if you ordain women, and you will lose them if you don't. That's a pragmatic argument, from one pastor to another. In the global north, your constituents have already adopted positive attitudes toward women and also contraception. I don't know about the global south. But I never met a woman, rich or poor, educated or not, who liked being put down and left out.

Neither of us is against pragmatism. We just don't want it to interfere with what is right. When something useful to you coincides with what is right, it's time to pay attention. Ordinary people don't want to follow a pope who compromises. Let's declare this argument as coming from the higher pragmatism.

The institution you represent isn't as antiwoman as it seems. Your members don't really believe that women are not in the line of Saint Peter or incapable of being called by the Almighty to sacred orders. Yes, I'm being a sneaky instrumentalist here, dragging in pragmatism where it doesn't belong. By the way, you are brilliant at dethroning pragmatism on every page of the encyclical. You want praise to replace pragmatism. That's why I respect you so much. I want to encourage you to praise the people who want to do the right thing—and who are fed up with spiritual leaders who don't do the right thing. I want you to go higher and deeper. And I think you have the stones to do it. Forgive the sexism.

We all have great respect for the institutional obstacles you face in ordaining women. I'm not saying it's easy; I'm saying it is right (as in *righteous*) because women are not objects, and right because you believe that God made the whole creation—including women. It also happens to be pragmatic. You take a great risk if you don't do the right thing. You could lose many admirers. I'm not one of the ones you'll lose; I'll stick with you. But I won't agree with you. And I will lose some, not all, respect for you. That is the sum of my argument.

Every good relationship should have some strong disagreements. Ours will, too. The best and most credible—nay, incredible—thing you could do for the environment would be to lift the ban on ordaining women, for that would show that you really mean that the environment and the economy are related. It would show that you refuse to otherize nature or women or any matter.

Philosophically, it would be a queer breakthrough, the kind that finally abolishes the stewardship-over-dominion fight. By "queer," I mean busting the binaries that bother us all so much. Queer is certainly pro-gay, but it is much more. It means getting over the versus problem, which you have identified as the fundamental problem that praise faces on its way to justice and beauty. In the versus world, we think of ourselves as disconnected and in need of protection. In the connected world, we see ourselves as connected and in need of deeper relationship. I think I'll write you a whole letter about queers.

The Obstacles

Let's rehearse the absurd ideas that keep your institution off the right track. Your boys Aquinas and Aristotle argue that only males can be priests because priests need to represent the entire human race. For some reason or another, only males perfectly model the human species. The inglorious roots of this weird dogma lie in Aquinas's view, adopted from Aristotle, that only men are "complete" humans. Women just don't measure up. Aquinas says women are *deficiens et occasinatus*—in English, "defective and misbegotten" or "unfinished and caused accidentally." Besides being untrue (God did create women, and we are fully human), this theology is the foundation of all the other otherizing. It puts a man against his own mother. You mercifully are the first pope to call earth "Mother Earth." Thank you. Your inner logic is pro-woman. I don't think you believe we are incomplete or defective or misbegotten. So why continue to keep us from ordination? I just want you to follow out your own thought and say good-bye to Aristotle and Aquinas and their otherizing.

There is great power in religious institutions to keep the new in labor and not to birth it. The cardinals still have power. They have residual power, real

estate powers, and the power of salaries and patron-
age. They have the ironically active power of inertia.
They have the power of desperation and the fear of
becoming obsolete. How will you manage these inter-
acting realities?

Although your remarkable events start and stop
on time and there's abundant evidence that you have
a great staff, you also seems to be winging it, the way
most spiritual entrepreneurs do. So, of course, is the
established institution of the Roman Catholic Church.
It is no different than other institutions in the early
twenty-first century in terms of the great disruptions
it—and we—face. The institution may appear sturdy,
but not if you assess its numbers, its spiritual vitality, or
the number of churches it is closing in every community. The institution may appear sturdy, but its loss of
credibility around the clergy-abuse crisis feels to many
souls akin to a deathblow. Even one soul lost to the
long-lasting horror of pedophilia is too much; instead,
there are thousands. The diminishment of institutional power is real—and the only thing more real is
the capacity of institutions to survive even as they lose
power. How will you manage this? Will you manage
it by not managing it? That would be your spiritual
logic, I'm guessing. The organization that pays you is

so weak. A slight push could change it. The old would fall away. The new is beating strong within.

You have the best theological argument. You argue brilliantly against the false biblical interpretation of dominion. Dominion means that awful interpretation, where man is over nature, as man is over women. We are in a theological fight for the planet here. You are my leader. I am following you—all the way to your deep inner self, the one who wants a real break with the past and its mistakes. You want to succeed at praising God's creation. So do I. We are going to have to take great risks to turn the trouble around. Let's go together. The only real obstacle is the human institution and its bad habits. In a certain way, compared with praising the truth, that's a very small obstacle.

The Hem of His Garment

Can we do another Bible study together? You handle the scriptures magnificently throughout *Laudato Si'* and in declaring the year of mercy. Let's go a little deeper into how the scriptures treat women and how women are portrayed in the scripture. (Another thing we Protestants believe is that we have to read our own scriptures and understand them together.)

These scriptures keep me curious about how much self-knowledge even Jesus had. "And they besought him that they might only touch the hem of his garment: and as many as touched were made perfectly whole" (Matthew 14:36 KJ21). "Just then a woman who had been subject to bleeding for twelve years came up behind him and touched the edge of his cloak" (Matthew 9:20 NIV). "She said to herself, 'If I only touch his cloak, I will be healed'" (Matthew 14:35 NIV). "And when the men of that place recognized Jesus, they sent word to all the surrounding country. People brought all their sick to him" (Matthew 14:35 NIV). "The people all tried to touch him, because power was coming from him and healing them all"(Luke 6:19 NIV).

Jesus didn't discriminate against women. And he often tried to give his power away. My curiosity doesn't really start with the woman part. After all, it was a woman who touched the hem of his garment and was healed. People didn't approve of Jews touching menstruating women, but that seems to be left out here. People also didn't seem to comment on his healing of a "woman." Instead, they let her be part of "healing them all." I wonder what you think is going on in these texts. I know they're about making Jesus look good. But what about that hem business? And that woman business?

I admit, I'm a little upset with this woman, just as I'm upset with the way your hem gets used and abused. I worry that you will take your power too seriously, rather than really spread it around, that you'll grow afraid of the institutional obstacles, which will dilute the power of your faith and hope. You will be less the leader than you could be.

I have been bothered by how many people want to borrow your power as opposed to build a movement. It's the hem thing. Even Jesus didn't overdo his healing miracle. He spread his power around and taught others to heal. You told people at the World Meeting of Families in 2015 in Philadelphia to stop touching your hem and go down the hall and knock on the door of the lonely woman that they usually avoid. I loved that speech and that statement. It told me you knew what you were doing. It told me you were real and really like Jesus. Not that you were Jesus, but that you were like him. You had the power in your hem—and you wanted us all to have that power of touching each other, too.

You were a street priest in Argentina, so you know what I mean. People want a passive Savior—one who makes it all right for them. That passivity will save neither people nor planet. As you well know, we have to get *everybody* involved in praising and loving God's creation. We don't need surrogates to do that for us; we need to do it ourselves, in a new kind of togetherness, the one beyond *versus*. I'm arguing for women's ordination and leadership, but I'm really arguing for a certain kind of leadership, one that empties and opens to all. It's a leadership that knows the power of its hem and refuses it, intentionally.

You have surely read Philippians 2, where God pours power into the earth and into Jesus. The one who was exalted is humbled, and the humbled one exalted. I love this passage, and I love the way you imitate it in your own behavior, in your car and your shoes, your deeply kenotic ways. Kenosis: the spending down of power, the heaven come to earth, spirit to flesh, valleys raised, mountains brought low of the incarnation.

You don't hoard power; you spread it around. Others, including me, are more powerful because of what you say and do. That's the Jesus way. It's not being puffed up by the touching of him or his hem, for that way belittles God's action in creation. It's a spiritual us *and* them, not a spiritual us versus them. The latter approach keeps us from the full-throated praise we have ready to go. It has hurt both the polar bears and us women very much.

As feminist Gloria Steinem says, "I don't want to pass on the torch. I want my own torch." I think you get this. Now you need to show us that you get it. You don't lose your torch by helping others have a torch. Have a great torch of your own, Francis. And then make sure others do, too.

Walking through the scriptures about the hem, I see people displacing power onto external authorities. They refuse the kenotic power and go for the hoarded power, the power of the "other"—even the other Jesus—to save them. The touch on the hem of Jesus' garment may have proved salvific for "many." But what about the people who never got to touch the hem? What about the ones you call the least of these? What happens to them as creation goes on and on in its familiar path, leaving so many behind?

Jesus argued, as you did in Philadelphia, that we have the power to heal ourselves and heal each other. That is the Protestant principle: the lateralization of power and authority. Protestants believe in the priesthood of all believers. Many women believe its truth—and yet are barred from the priesthood.

You told people to stop trying to touch you and go touch the lonely woman down the hall. You told us to touch each other. I think you meant it. I think you're pretty queer yourself, more like a mother tree than a father pope.

Back to Philadelphia

When you went to Philadelphia, you had a very insightful point of view on the family. You reached for the consensus, the epiphany that we join together in seeking.

"The family is under assault, internally and externally," you said. Instead of being a scold, you showed appreciation for those who try to stay in families assaulted by months too long for the money. This insight joins Republican to Democrat and vice versa. It acknowledges that personal responsibility joins public failure in making a mess out of things. It's a more wholesome theology, because it joins individual sin to social sin. It also stops blaming the poor for their poverty and blaming "mothers" for being the sole source of trouble in the family. As has now become your normal and usual, you bridge. *Dialogue* is your favorite word, I think.

I agreed with your nuanced assessment of the family, only to be thrown a serious liturgical curve ball in Philadelphia. What happened in Mass didn't jibe with what you were saying about the family.

I got my tickets way in advance. I was proud of my planning to see you. I left New York to continue my quest for you with a full heart. I was a new convert. I sensed that I was touching something holy, even though I am Protestant enough to know that touching is a little like magical thinking. Miracles are one thing for us Enlightenment-bred people who don't go back as far as you do. Magical thinking is just too pagan.

You anticipated my concern when you told people at the Mass in Philadelphia not to touch you but to find the lady down the hall that no one touches and everyone avoids. "Touch her," you said, in a way that imitated Jesus' constant deflection of attention from himself to others or to his Abba. Of all the things you have said so far, this sending us down the hall is my favorite, as I think you have figured out by now.

Thus, the liturgical mess that happened in Philly really mattered to me. It was so full of dissonance. At the Holy Mass at the World Meeting of Families 2015 in Philadelphia, I was impressed with your theological consistency about touching and about what Ross Douthat of the *New York Times* called your "ostentatious humility." Still, there I was, watching you surrounded by dozens of men distributing the Mass. It bugged me. I hated to be so gender conscious and so disturbed by those who were a part of the Mass. And then it hit me: Of course you were celebrating Mass with men! They're your team. They're your disciples. They're your staff. Women may also have been involved, and surely there were some tokens around, doing seemingly important things. A woman had been in charge of the art for the cathedral (she was much touted in the press), but no woman was at the table. None was even close. I perused the videos afterward, only to see man after man after man. I was told after my questioning that the shots were all wrong, that indeed some women were close. At this point, I don't think I care.

Worshipping, watching, listening to the marvelous antiphon by Julian Darias Revie of the Yale School of Music helped. I decided I needed to get into the music because all the men were giving me the creeps. I didn't want to be a counter, but I felt excluded. Once you try to worship and can't because you can't stop noticing all the men in the room and the absence of women, you just get weird. I couldn't worship with so much negative energy inside. I felt as if I didn't belong. I was being excluded by something in which I wanted to be included. I was that Lutheran girl again being asked by the bishop of Virginia, before being rejected for Lutheran ordination, "Do you think you have gender-related identity problems?" You bet I do!

Called "The Love of God," Revie's antiphon was quiet and well paced. It soothed me. I knew the love of God was not genderized or gender specific. I could tell the music was telling me that God loves me. I just didn't know why one like me wasn't standing at the holy table. It was like being invited to a dinner party but not being given a plate or a knife or a fork, much less any food. It was painful, especially for me, your new convert.

I had been in this moment before. I was area minister (one with episcopal responsibilities) for the United Church of Christ in the 1990s. It was like being the human resources department for 125 churches. I was invited to the installation of the new Catholic bishop for western Massachusetts. We Protestants were all decked out in the front row. A rope was put across the row so we didn't make the mistake of going up during the Mass. I climbed over the fence and took Communion. The ushers were flabbergasted. Many of my associates did the same thing.

Something is telling me that there is a fence to climb again right now—and the fence is not what you first think. It's not about getting our anger right against religious institutions that disappoint us by being against us in ways both subtle and formal. It is instead about self-protecting cynicism. Why not climb over into the hope of an expanded table? You have that hope in your heart. So do I. Why let a few fences and a couple thousand years get in the way? I'm going to try to hop the fence of my self-protecting cynicism and hope.

I'm pretty sure that your inclusive theology will ultimately cause you to ordain women. I don't know how you will, but I believe you will. Your inner logic will follow the music in your soul. Your being saved—as in totally secure—will help you along.

I don't think you will change on abortion, because another inner logic prevails there. It is the logic of the seamless cloth or fabric of life. I don't need to agree with you on abortion. In a new interreligious world, surely many will have different viewpoints on the beginning and the end of life. As long as we have constitutional protections—and you Catholics and Evangelicals stop allowing their religious power to be politically abused—I have no problem with different moral voices on different moral matters.

With these thoughts and more, I consoled myself during the Philadelphia Mass. They are only ideas at this point. But they are the ones I have because of the trust I have in the leader who is not afraid.

I also am not that afraid. It would break my heart if you missed the opportunity to open the world to women but I knew that could happen when I first started loving you. I've been heartbroken before. I simply have to fuss with you about and for women. We are not an extra issue. We might even be *the* issue, creating a paradigm shift towards ecological integrity. For example, the small change of allowing women who have had abortions to receive forgiveness, if they apply for it within a year, is an action that diminished you. Abortion is not a sin to many of them, so why should they have to request forgiveness—or even ask for forgiveness for not believing they had sinned in the first place? And making incremental change (while loving the whole cloth of forgiveness) and limiting the forgiveness to one year is arbitrary. What if a woman asks for forgiveness on day 366? Or had two abortions and asks for forgiveness for only one?

You didn't ask me for advice, but I'll give it anyway, as a disciple of your movement at a much simpler level. If you make administrative compromises on momentous issues, like whether to ordain women, you'll lose adherents. You will lose authority with the disaffected masses you are trying to reach—and you'll only please the insiders, those who have only their track record of destroying the church's credibility on which to stand. You will have to decide whether you are working for the insiders or the outsiders, for Jesus and his incarnation or for the institution that has failed to be his body.

Jesus showed us how to touch both our own power and each other. He also argued powerfully that the church is his body. We are not Jesus. You are not Jesus either. You are giving Jesus a good name. We want to follow you. We want to follow you in such a way that we find ourselves saved and powerful. We have inherited the power to touch each other. That is the mystery of the incarnation and of Jesus, being among us and then leaving us behind. His resurrection is actually in our touch, in our hands and our feet. That kind of touch, the one we learn from the one who refrained from getting all puffed up about his power—that kind of touch is not magical. It is a miracle. It is something you can share with women, too.

For you to be as new as you can be, especially in your love of a just environmental economy, you must ordain women. You will have to make sure that people are not just fixated on your hem or your touching it. You will have to show us how to touch each other. If I had that task, I'd absolutely want some women on my team. Women aren't necessarily better than men at the art of touch or healing, but we are damn good at it. If you do not kenotically pour power into earth and us, your refrain will put the lie to all the rest. This is not just a pragmatic matter, either. It's a spiritual matter, involving what is true about Jesus and about touch and about scripture and about you and me.

A Small and Simple Theology of Ordination

Not everyone should be ordained. But no one should be refused ordination because of their orientation or their gender. That exclusion diminishes ordination and turns it into the very thing it is not. It is a sacred, not a banal, quality and calling. Cardinal Leo Joseph Suenens is often remembered as saying, "Remember, God has called you to the priesthood because he does not trust you to be a layman." I am not elevating ordination when I get enthusiastic about ordination. There are lots of very fine people, perhaps especially nuns, who don't need the mantle or mark of ordination. However, making it off limits to women, when men are failing so brilliantly at their calls, is ridiculous. And wrong.

I would like you to get to know and really listen to Sister Joan Chittister, arguably the strongest woman's voice expanding your message while directly questioning it. Of course, Mary Hunt is great, too. I have been a subscriber to her newsletter, *Water*, for decades now. I think you'd love her because you are so nuts about water, too. Anyway, I suggest these two sages because I know you have no real reason to listen to me. I'm not in your system. I am just one of your fans and proud to be one.

Joan just gave the fiftieth-anniversary speech at the *National Catholic Reporter anniversary celebration*. Standing in that long line of unordained women who are Catholic leaders, like Dorothy Day and Mother Theresa, she has refused to go away.

Sister Joan loves to tell a joke about a guy going into the bar, repeatedly asking for grapes, and the bar owner finally throws him out, shouting, "We don't have any grapes; we only have booze!" I love to reinterpret her story. She tells it a lot. It's about the wine in the grapes, for sure, but also about people's hunger for a holy sacrament. I respect the Catholic point of view that the bread and the wine are good even if the priest isn't. I also don't think Sister Joan or Mother Teresa or Saint Dorothy needed to be ordained. They did not. I think instead that the fact they *cannot* or *could not* be ordained puts the lie to more than itself. Lying about the holy discredits the holy. What is the lie? That women aren't human enough to preside at the holy table. Jesus thought we were human enough to touch. What do you really think?

Your institution—but not your faith, nor your Jesus—has long had a hard time with female power. However, I believe we—the songbirds or the sea or the people or the planet—wouldn't be in so much trouble right now if people could have seen the full humanity of women. I think your own inner logic agrees.

Joan of Arc was murdered for wearing men's pants. I certainly don't want women murdered, nor do I think ordained women need to wear men's pants. We need to find our own way. We need to transform what we mean by power and hems and healing. We need to participate in our salvation.

The biggest issue we both have to face is whether the church's sacraments actually represent the Jesus it loves and remembers. "You got any grapes?" is a really good question. Is the sacrament itself profaned by the exclusion of women? I fear the answer is yes.

Women are bioneers, sacramentally as well as spiritually as well as politically as well as environmentally. You have the power to give us a chance. I hope you will use it.

The Holy Grail and a Thread Talk

One of the most profound events of my life had to do with the hosting of the Women of the Grail, a French order, which had a base in Ohio. They brought together the first generation of ordained women in my denomination every summer, as a gift to us. We went to their farm in Grailville, Ohio, and spent a week talking

to each other. These nuns so wanted us Protestants to
succeed that they gathered us for fun and friendship.
Nights we went into their swimming hole for skinny-
dipping. Days we lived in their made-over barns in
relatively comfortable beds. We served each other
the Eucharist, sometimes in a rare kind of ecstasy. We
wrote in Burma Shave on the bathroom windows after
showers, "Resurrection Lurking." We spent the days
theologizing and reading Mary Daly's book *Beyond God
the Father*. We read about three pages a day, so interested
were we in getting it right.

You have created a platform as good as Grailville,
as kenotic as it was, for us Protestants. You have also
shared that platform with people who aren't Christians,
including women who aren't Christians. You have a
chance at helping us all respect each other. Like the nun
who rode by on her tractor, in her habit, right before
breakfast at Grailville, you have a chance to spread the
good around. She did it in her own way. You will also
in your own way. You follow the holy grail, the thread
that binds us to both past and future. Get grailing!

Love,
Donna

5

Dear Francis,
I Think You're Queer

Dear Francis,

I think you are queer. I mean that as a compliment, an appreciation, and a way to continue to hold you in high regard. By queer, I mean having a theology that is versus versus or against against or unwilling to be divided into parts. I'm describing wholeness, particularly wholeness of gender. I mean both/and. I mean life beyond the double bind of the double binary. (You have met the either/ors: either you are this, or you are that—a girl or a boy, a man or a woman, a Republican or a Democrat, a Sunni or a Shia, a Catholic or a Protestant, good or bad, rich or poor, white or black.) I mean that same proud claim of humanity that you speak of when you praise creation. You have a great sense of the all, the whole, the way the parts fit together. We might even accuse you of a Lego kind of humanity: you believe we all fit into something we can build together.

By queer, I also mean what my father tried to mean when he said, "He is as queer as a two-dollar bill." What my father meant was not a compliment. It was a slur, a way of saying that because some man was behaving in an effeminate way, he wasn't normal; he was another kind of dollar, an abnormal kind of dollar. When I bring up this slur, I do so as a way of flipping it. I have a large collection of two-dollar bills. They do exist now, and it's kind of fun to use them. People like them; cashiers smile when you hand them one. They especially like them when you say they are legitimate, which they are. My whole congregation is full of two-dollar bills. My whole congregation, gay and straight and bi and trans, is as queer as a two-dollar bill, and that's why I love it so much.

When I was a young mother and a young minister, I often went to the Riverhead, New York, clergy breakfasts on Fridays. We met in a nice Greek diner. There were five of us in town, and we enjoyed one another's company. The other four were men. Once, my then-four-year-old son, Isaac, was too sick to go to school but not too sick to go out with me to this breakfast. He sat there in that pre-fever daze of a child with yet another earache, cuddled against my down coat and picking away at his French toast. He started poking me and insisted on whispering something in my ear: "Mommy, boys can't be ministers."

Everybody heard him, and we all had a good laugh. What I have always loved about the ministry is how androgynous it is. You get to be a boy and a girl, a man and a woman, by role. The androgyny goes deeper: the men wear vestments that could be mistaken for dresses; the women are often accused of being out of our place, because the ministry implies some kind of authority. Many people think of priests as either too effeminate or too masculine or somehow "queer." That's one of the main reasons I think being a minister is the best work in the world. You're just a little outside the gender boxes. Nobody quite knows what to make of you.

By queer, I mean refusing to be doubled in anybody else's bind. I have a friend who says queering is a refusal to be otherized as normal or abnormal. Not one, not the other, but neither and therefore both. You, Francis, are a little normal and a little abnormal. Your gender is mixed. It is wonderfully complete and slightly odd. I think you are queer, too.

Picking a Fight

In the name of our mutual and precious queering, I want to quarrel with you about celibacy. I just don't get it. I love orgasm and tenderness and physical intimacy way too much to imagine they aren't holy. I also think celibacy has led to the rampant pedophilia in your world. But isn't it unqueer of me to want everybody to want the kind of intimacy I want? I don't know why I would or should care so much about celibacy. Obviously it makes me so uncomfortable that I become one of those people who enforces her sexuality on other people. So do you mind if I muse for a while and try to keep my finger from wagging at you?

I worry that pedophilia, so rampant among priests, is a problem stemming from a longing. Many people don't share this worry, I know. Of course, there are sexually active people who are also involved in pedophilia; not just celibate priests. Having sex with children is more than problematic. It is wrong. But I can't help thinking that those skirts worn by presumably celibate

priests cloak power as much as they authorize difference. It is just common sense to think that. Sex without
consent or the possibility of consent is wrong.

In addition, I join many people in thinking of celibacy as a spiritual practice that has failed to ping spiritually. Yes, it has set people apart. Yes, it shows a kind
of devotion to spirit over matter. Surely, many find it
a beautiful experience, one chosen and weighted with
commitment. Surely, not all celibate people are sexually predatory. But still: I don't get celibacy. I am sorry
to say it. I just don't get why God would want people not to physically love each other. Maybe you can
explain it to me?

I find denial in general an odd route to God. In my
world, so many people deny themselves so much. They
may overdo sexual expression and freedom, but they
simultaneously deny each other respect or quiet or freedom from other people's put-downs. I am probably very
much more open to a spiritual denial, like fasting or even
celibacy, than I am open to denial for denial's sake. If I
could understand what celibacy was affirming, I could
probably get closer to understanding what it is denying.

I don't think pedophilia is just a priestly problem.
Sexual predation is also alive and well in my world.
Adultery, pornography, having affairs with someone

in our youth group, someone less a child and more a teen—these are our abnormals. I have to take a boundary-training course every year or lose my standing. I also have to pay $235 for an annual background check. Why? Because there have been so many lawsuits against clergy in my denomination—lawsuits that people have won—that all of us have to pay for extra insurance protection. The insurance companies won, and I am deeply insulted by having to pay this money and take these courses. It's like medical-malpractice insurance that you have to pay for even if you are not malpracticing.

The courses, by the way, repeat one thing over and over: don't have sexual relations with your parishioners. I may not like the rule of celibacy, and I surely don't like many rules. But this one is so obvious that I don't think I need to be hit over the head with it all the time. Still, all this fussing on my part is nothing compared with the huge heartbreak people experience when one of us "steps out" and over a sexual boundary.

The courses also assure us that sexual predation or violence is not about sex so much as it is about power. If we use the power of our office to hurt others, we have crossed a boundary, caused harm, and denied the holiness of our office. I agree with this power idea. It applies to rape, too. What's wrong about rape is the way it uses power and prohibits consent. I know more about rape than you'll want to know, having cofounded the first women's organization against rape. We trained police and hospital emergency rooms not to blame the woman who was just raped and came for help. Women Organized Against Rape (WOAR) became a national organization. We knew rape was about power, not about sex. So please help me connect celibacy to powerlessness and not predation. I am trying to understand.

I remember the first time one of my parishioners told me she had been incested, over and over again, as a child. Her uncle seemed to think he had a right to all of C's siblings as well. C died single at age sixty-eight, after helping me raise Isaac and volunteering in our church office every weekday afternoon from one to five. She had retired from being a cleaning lady at the local college. She lived in low-income housing, had never had sexual relations that were consensual, and didn't believe that God really loved her. She kept to her tangled self-image about being unlovable till the day she died. From C, I learned several things. The main one is that the damage done by abuse, especially of a child, is far more than just physical. It is also spiritual. It damages our spiritual muscles. Just when we were supposed to be tendered and protected, we got the opposite. We were used.

Sometimes the damage is forever. It also was for M, a woman whose Catholic parents together abused her, regularly, in a cult ritual. She just doesn't think she is worthy. I'm no developmental psychologist, but I know the early stages in life are when trust begins. Without that first trust, it is very, very hard to go on to the next life stages. M is stuck being unable to trust without enormous effort. She trusts someone every now and then episodically. Why is it so hard for her? Because of pedophilia, better called child sexual abuse. You don't love a child when you sexually touch her or him. Child sexual abuse is not a small sin. It is a sin that keeps on harming.

Interestingly, these two painful cases are just two of many that have broken my pastoral heart. They have nothing to do with priests or celibacy or pedophilia. They are violence done by so-called ordinary hetero-sexuals to their own family members. But in my relationship with you, it is hard to ignore the mounting evidence of pedophilia in the priesthood. And many think of the priesthood as fatherly, as intimate, as foun-dational to trust. When pedophilia is on the front page of the paper, causing insurance rates for the clergy to go up and people to be appalled at priests and ministers, it attacks fundamental trust, not just sexual organs.

I wonder so often about your own childhood. I can tell someone helped you learn to trust yourself and others. You have been a son, a brother, and an uncle. You've never been a parent. You probably don't want to be a parent. It is overrated as a vocation, especially since there are so many of us who are so terrible at it or who don't get near the resources we need to provide for our offspring in the first place or have seen how overpopulated the world is. Never even mind whether we build trust in children at the appropriate stage or give them enough to eat! (My second son, Jacob, the twin to my queer daughter, is about to adopt a child. It will cost him $25,000. Then why adopt? There are just way too many children in the world, says he.) I'm surely not enforcing parenthood when I misunderstand celibacy. *Misunderstand* is the right word: I just don't understand celibacy.

There is a lot about humans and sexuality that I don't understand. And I find that many of my days are spent sitting with people who are more than confused. They want help navigating the sexual paths and patterns—those that lead to parenthood and those that don't. I am sure you learned about gender and what a real man really is. I wonder how you handle skipping out on the lesson about power and consent and being different. Probably nobody else ever told you the kinds of things they told me, like, "Isn't that skirt too short for church?" I had no idea what they meant until much later. Now I know. The message was that my sexuality was not godly or churchly and that I'd better figure out some unholy place in which to express it while fulfilling my duties to procreate.

I wonder if you ever want to disobey instructions? I know I do. This late in my life, I am developing the goal of being a rogue, someone who lives outside the instructions long enough to feel what it is like. I have been a wife, mother, daughter, sister. I have been a pastor, pastor, pastor. I have no interest in abandoning any of these roles, as they satisfy me. I just want to know who Donna is in there, underneath all the roles and all the gender roles and all the questions that still follow her around. I wonder if I've taken all the risks I could have taken and said all the outrageous things I've thought of saying. I suppose Tina Fey and Amy Poehler and Samantha Bee are encouraging me. Why do I want to be like those actresses? Because they are women who have gone rogue. They are funny. They are irreverent. Someone asked Amy Poehler if she was surprised how successful her comedy had become. She answered, "No." She's not ashamed of being rogue. She and her pals have abandoned the normal humilities about women and the normal self-refusals.

I sense that you able to be humble about being yourself. There is no question you are a rogue pope. I sense very little shame in you. I wonder how you got that way—so delightfully queer in the middle of a very strange organization.

It's Not Just Celibacy

I also want to quarrel with you about your institution's commandment to keep sex procreative as opposed to recreative. This argument will have to turn on the same queer assumption: I am not against you for encouraging your adherents to want to have one kind of sex. I just want to make sure you make space for differences and other ways to be moral about sex—as in procreative and recreative, as opposed to only one way.

Sex is fun. When my son Isaac, the one with the precocity and the ear infection, turned twelve, he remained precocious. He came home from seventh grade and asked if I could give him the lowdown on sex, and if I could do it quickly. He was like that in his adolescent questions: very authoritative, way too

early. I said sure, though quaking inside. I knew that he
already knew how to do it. So I quipped, "Sex is good
when both people say yes, when nobody gets hurt,
and when you only have the babies you want. In other
words, use protection against birth until you're ready
for a baby." He said thanks and went up to his room.

I was changing his sheets a few days later, and on
the wall next to his bed, he had written, "Everybody
says yes, nobody gets hurt, no babies," in his boyish
handwriting. I still I have the note he wrote to himself.

Francis, you and I could talk a long time about what
kind of sexual person you are and want to be. And I
could talk a long time about how I am morally and
spiritually prepared to be the kind of sexual person I
am. I think we're both capable of being queer. Meaning: we could be even better queers if we decided not to
fight about sex or convince each other about celibacy
or abortion or procreation or homosexuality. So let's be
so good at being queer that we refuse to reform each
other. I'm not trying to reform you or convince you
to ordain gays or women or stop celibacy or even to
accuse you of not doing enough about pedophilia. That
is actually ungay. If queer means the place beyond the
binary of straight and gay, or means that we refuse to be
against things or versus things or people, then I have to

act without controlling you. I can use all the authority in my power to be me and say me and keep my ideas in a closet. But I can't force you to change. That would be the kind of thingifying of the other that we queers finally object to, with all the wholeness that we have.

I do want to differentiate and honor our differences. I love you, as I have said over and over again. I think I know why you do what you do. But I'm not sure you know why I do what I do. Since we're both Christians and read pretty much the same Bible, maybe some articulation of difference will help us be better queers. I wish you would change your church. I won't stop loving you if you don't. There is just way too much good in you for me to position what's not so good against you. Plus, who am I to judge?

You and the Religious Right

Right and left are so unqueer as concepts that it's embarrassing to bring them up. Yet we live in a hardened world where these differences have taken on extraordinary power and done extraordinary harm. Suffering is one thing; unnecessary suffering is another. The hardening of the enemies against each other is unnecessary suffering.

Queers often say, "Don't be mean." My daughter, Katie, who says she is queer, who lives with a woman and would also proudly identify as lesbian, asked me what I was going to get her four-year-old niece (my four-year-old granddaughter) for her birthday. Eva Juliet is her name, and she is into pink. I don't mean just a little into pink. I mean a refusal to eat out of anything but a pink bowl or to wear anything but a pink princess dress, along with an insistence on carrying around a pink purse all day long. Katie, who is way smarter than I'll ever be on the meaning of the word *queer*, said she was trying to figure out whether to go minimal princess, medium princess, or maximal princess. I was astonished. She said, "Eva likes princesses because they don't look like any girl she has ever seen. They are different, and they make her different." I thought that was a really good answer. We both went into maximal princess territory for our gifts.

I'm going to follow her way here and try not to be mean, though I'm afraid I will fail. The Religious Right has been so mean to me and mine that I find myself predisposed to meanness. I know Jesus refused to have an enemy. So do I refuse. But I fail in that refusal. Father, forgive me. And help me repent my foolish ways.

The Religious Right has turned blame and shame into political power, using their moralistic bludgeons especially on people who have sex for recreational purposes, as though this evolution in human sexuality were not good for the planet. It's almost as if they added an eleventh commandment to their phony literalism about the gospel: "Thou shalt procreate." The subconscious here is protecting the biology of the human. Fine, but as we all know, young human beings are more interested in the pleasure of sex than in procreation. Evolution comes in quietly. We don't know how it works as much as we know it does work. We need to stop having so many children. You know it, and I know it, but oddly, we seem to think that poor people are the ones who should lead the way. Now, that is mean.

More and more children are being born intersex. I firmly believe this is evolution dialoguing with culture and that trans is becoming a biological as well as a cultural fact. According to the Intersex Society of North America, between one in fifteen hundred and one in two thousand babies are born noticeably atypical in terms of genitalia, so much so that a specialist in sex differentiation is called in. Likewise, we know that about one out of ten people know quite early that they are "gay." Isn't that wonderful? Especially for you and me and our appreciation of evolution and biodiversity and hybridity?

I've confessed that I am pretty constantly angry with the Religious Right, many of whom are Catholics. But you should know that I'm equally judgmental about the Religious Left. The Religious Left also turns blame and shame into political power: "You can't be using plastic bags." "You aren't driving a Prius?" Catastrophism is the theory of the environmental movement, buoyed by underground fears that we are just plain wrong about everything, including our own evolutionary stake. We're more than convinced that we should reproduce less. There is absolutely no evidence that progressives have more fun with sex than conservatives, but at least we feel less guilty about the fun we do have. However, we share the same basic theological muscle of shame and blame. Right blames Left, which blames Right, which blames Left. I'm not having fun yet.

At the heart of the environmental movement is a certain catastrophism. If you don't shape up, you will die. You may die pre-hell, but hell on this side is just as obnoxious as hell on the other side. The Right, while protecting reproduction from fun or freedom, also enjoys a catastrophism. You'll go to hell if you have an abortion. Isn't it odd that both movements—and their multiple and multiplying variants—fear hell and don't hear the call from heaven? And both get all unsexy about sex, pretty much all the time. I can't do anything about the Right. I can do something about the catastrophism of the Left.

I want to differ with you about our queerness on behalf of our larger project. Again, your inner spiritual logic is accepting of all people. "Who am I to judge?" We would have so much more fun if we would pull our institutions along. You have at least three more years or 1,056 days to be pope. When do you think we can hope for an announcement about ordaining queers? Would I be amiss to think that most of the people you have already ordained are queer, if not gay?

The stakes are very high. The entire environmental and economic project hinges on these matters. It will fail if we don't lose our judgment and adopt our queerness with joy. Ordinary people who like sex will remain suspicious of any religion that doesn't join them erotically. Until the religious and political Left abandons shame-and-blame theology in approaching sex first and the environmental crisis second, the public will remain confused and the environment unprotected.

Punishmentalists on the Left are environmental catastrophists, causing fear instead of hope. Punishmentalists on the Right are sexual catastrophists, causing fear instead of hope. The Right punishes sex; the Left punishes cars. It's the same spiritual muscle being used. We seem to need an enemy, and usually it is you for me and me for you. Queering that matter would go a long way to make for more protection for the environment that we might yet praise and love and allow to amuse us.

We may think we will be politically successful, like the Right, using fear, but we will not change the spiritual environment, which is ultimately more important than carbon reductions. To return Christianity to its humbler and holier roots, in hope and grace, rather than shame and blame, is the evolutionary task of today. We could joyfully side with our biology and be less catastrophic in our care of the earth. We might even re-create and regenerate and have more re-creational sex, on our way to resanctifying the desanctified. Richard Rohr— joining many others, including you—argues well that the root issue is the reenchantment of the disenchanted. Why not break free of the catastrophic sticks and opt for the enchanting carrots?

Which is more spiritually and politically useful, a carrot or a stick? The answer is probably a little bit of both. The Left could distinguish itself and deepen itself spiritually by using more carrots and fewer sticks. You, as pope, have so much power here. The power is restraint, in refraining from judgment. Surely you have bigger fish to fry than punishing gay people or keeping them from having sex if they are priests.

The real danger to the environment is public confusion, not adequate metrics nor political will. The confusion is based in the punishmental cul de sac: how can we right what is wrong without destroying our motivation to improve? Religious formation plays an enormous part in how we perceive what we cannot know. How can we be good and help the earth? That's the question. How can we have fun and help the earth? How can we look at 2066 with great joy and hope in our eyes? For me, the place of hope is exactly where you find it: in queering the polarizations of all kinds and praising the earth. Everyone says yes, nobody gets hurt, and you have the babies you want.

We Don't Need to Quarrel

Clergy get to meet great people, especially around weddings. When Denise and Peter married in our sanctuary in Riverhead, there were no dogs officially in the wedding, as that was against church policy. The two dogs that showed up unofficially must have thought they were in San Francisco, as they were wearing flowers in their hair. Town Supervisor Joe Janowski lent the couple his convertible for their getaway car. He was the same town supervisor who had prohibited our soup kitchen from starting a community garden and farmers' market in town because, he claimed, "It will never work." (Tell every chamber of commerce in the country that. Farmers' markets have been extraordinarily successful, even though lots of people were sure they couldn't possibly work. The point is, most of us are too pessimistic. Most of us don't have enough friends across the aisle of our politics. I wonder what people think won't work now? Gay ordination in the Roman Catholic Church? Married priests?)

Anyway, Joe was not known for his forward-looking point of view. Like our trustees, he did what he could with what he had. We both lived in the moment, while the future created itself without our consent. In a funny way, the church policies are pretty much always being violated and not just around having dogs at weddings.

Peter, then a contractor and a tile shop owner, likes to tell the story of laying tile on a job site while a plumber did the plumbing. The plumber started trash-talking a lesbian women. Peter announced, "Shut the F up; my wife is a lesbian." She was indeed a lesbian, and a town council member, long before people decluttered their closets with old-fashioned eyes. This tidbit about his wife explains why it was so nice that Joe, who didn't believe in farmers' markets or gay councilwomen, let them borrow his car for their wedding getaway. Yes, Denise was gay and then became straight. She met Peter at a bar in Polishtown. Now she and Peter run the newspaper for Riverhead, after doing many other interesting jobs and being many other interesting people on their way to carrying phones that go straight to the fire and police departments, so they can get the news out quick. They also have two beautiful daughters together. Nobody got hurt, everybody agreed, unofficially, and two babies were born.

Heteronormative families are *not* the wave of the future, Francis. And we both love families, right? And we share a sense that more is possible than most people think.

Queer people, like us, understand authority differently than most people do. We love multiple positions and possibilities. We rarely say anything is wrong or abnormal or "won't work." Instead, we could just say, "Tell me more."

An Important Book and an Important Appreciation: Queer Theorists Love You

Queer people like to unknow rather than know. Author Jack Halberstam traces a type of unknowing in *The*

Queer Art of Failure. Halberstam notes that if the current model of production is leading us toward ecosocial destruction and planetary catastrophe, then perhaps the best thing we can do is to cultivate failure. Whitney Bauman is an associate professor of religious studies at Florida International University, where he deals with issues of religion, nature, and queer theory. He loves you. He calls the kind of failure Halberstam writes about "experimental worlding." I think you are doing a lot of experimental worlding, even with a twinkle in your eye. Bauman said, in a lecture:

> Received and established knowledge helps us to order the world in a preconceived way in which newness becomes interpreted as more of the same; and second, that there is something about unknowing, uncertainty, and even failure that helps us to cultivate a form of listening in which the voices of previously unheard planetary realities come into speech and can then contribute toward new ways of being/becoming in the world. Thus, when we look at shifts in knowledge that transform the worlds in which we live, these shifts come as a result of paying attention to that which is made abject by received traditions.

Both of our institutions seem to be doing really well at failing—like, really well. What could you do to punish pedophile priests enough? Two hundred boys over a forty-year period in a Bavarian choir? Or the way Roman Catholics in authority fired Father Charles Curran and said he couldn't teach at Catholic universities because he held it was possible to dissent from the church's so-called infallibility?

If we head toward being more queer and less right and wrong, more queer and less good and bad, our destination is actually fallibility. I'd like to go there with you and talk about what I don't know. I'd love it if we could share how important our failures to fit into the "way things are" or "the real world" have been.

Another example of trying to be so right that you end up wrong: Cardinal Ratzinger stripped Seattle archbishop Raymond Hunthausen, a friend of mine from antiwar days, of much of his authority after he allowed gay Catholics to celebrate mass at Saint James Cathedral and allowed Catholic hospitals in his diocese to perform contraceptive sterilizations. Shortly after this removal of authority, Ratzinger declared homosexuality an "intrinsic moral evil."

Patricia Miller, another friend of mine, writes about you all the time. She is beyond appalled. Recently, in *Religion Dispatches*, she said, "Until the Vatican acknowledges the extent to which progressives were scapegoated to mask the church's own unresolved incongruences regarding sex, asking it to police anyone on abuse may be wishful thinking."

So, no matter how queer you are or how much fun we could be having together, unworlding and reworlding, making mistakes and joining the human race, there remain some heavy-duty matters surrounding your wish not to judge. Even I can't refrain from judgment about some matters, like choirboys and public humiliations of decent people. Forgive me, again, Father, for I have sinned.

Listen to Your Own Self

Oddly, as I was writing this chapter in February 2016, you got into a tussle with presidential candidate Donald Trump. He accused you of being political, and you said that indeed you were political because politics are useful to stopping poverty and protecting creation. You were on a plane coming back from Mexico. You also said that you no longer wanted to pay so much attention to civil unions. You wanted to give all your attention to poverty. I will stop scolding you—and yours—now. You're on your way to something coherent and connected. I thank you.

You know how to hope. You know how to pope. You know how to change. You know how to listen. In *Laudato Si'*, you encouraged us: "Yet all is not lost. Human beings, while capable of the worst, are also capable of rising above themselves, choosing again what is good, and making a new start."

Yes, you are very queer, not normal like the institution at all. I so wish you could meet my grown son Isaac and his three children. Isaac is now thirty-two. His whole family looks normal on the outside, but they are so much better than that. They are even successful in worldly terms. But what I like about them the most is how queer they are. Isaac is married to a rabbi. He walks around Brooklyn wearing a T-shirt that says, "My Mom Is a Minister, My Wife Is a Rabbi, Get over It." Consider what Isaac's son Caleb, age six, said to his teacher about what he wants to do when he grows up: "I want to be a daddy." It's thrilling to me to have a feminist for a grandson. I know lots of women who want to be mommies. I know very few boys who want to be daddies. Caleb also speaks beautiful Hebrew and prays well in his second language.

Here is my prayer for Caleb and for your many nonbiological children as well:

> Surprise us, O God, with a future for Caleb that we cannot yet imagine. Down the road, let us hope that Caleb's own offspring want to know what racism is or what settlements were in Israel or whether it was really true that women used to do all the housework or child raising or couldn't be rabbis, like Grandma. Hear, with us, the joy of Caleb's children being blessed with good air, manageable debt, good topsoil, and absurd genetic diversity in plant and animal.
>
> Let him always sleep when he is drowsy, but let him usually be artistically, politically, psychologically, and spiritually awake. Let him refuse domination and enjoy freedom. Let him be queer.
>
> Let the fresh start he enjoys in these early days always be a possibility for him, and when he dies, let him go to the ancient love, which mimics the love his family has for him, and which has long awaited his return. Amen.

I so wish you could meet Caleb. He is a lot of fun and likes to play birdie, a game where we use words to get rid of monsters that might be hiding in our bedrooms.

Caleb always wants to use his special powers. I am teaching him that his special powers might be words—and also trying as a person to join you in getting rid of monsters in our bedrooms.

Love,
Donna

6

Dear Francis, Bono Was Right: God Is Not a Captive of Religion

Dear Francis,

It's time for us to talk about what's really important: whether God is God. I didn't used to understand what Christians mean when we say, "Jesus Christ is Lord." I was afraid we meant that Christ was the only God and that other peoples' gods weren't really divine. Now I say for myself, devotionally, that Jesus is Lord, meaning that for me there is nothing bigger. I don't believe

Jesus is the Christ or the only way to God or that there is an only way to God. By Christ, I mean what many mean: that Jesus is the One God or True God or Only Real God. I believe instead that there are many spokes on the great wheel, many grails underground grailing, many ways and routes to God. God is like a deep underground river with multiple tributaries, connected and fairly invisible to my one small eye. I love the idea that God is not captive to my one small eye, my one small vision, time or space, birthday or birthplace, time zone or climate zone. I love the idea that God's Spirit shows up lots of places in lots of ways. You could say I am a complete relativist, and you would be right. I am. I love the many faces of God. If you want someone to be deliberate about difference, I'm your girl. I marvel at the size of God—and how I can't capture him or her or it.

When I pray in public, I pray, "God, you whom some call Allah and others call Jesus, and others call Christ and others call Breath, and others call Yahweh and others call Ruach, and others call force and others refuse to name, you who are beyond any form of human language of captivity, draw near. Bless us each and all on our way to you." I find great resonance in multiple communities to this prayer. It's freeing and at its core stops war and starts community.

Bono agrees with me, even though he also thinks Jesus is the Son of God. I no longer use that language, just because it's so laden with imperialism. It is fat with its own prideful correctness. Christians have ruined our language about God. Here's how Bono has put it in many different contexts:

"Sometimes religion gets in the way of God."

"To be one, to be united, is a great thing. But to respect the right to be different is maybe even greater."

"Even though I'm a believer, I still find it really hard to be around other believers. They make me nervous, they make me twitch. I sorta watch my back."

"We're starting our own religion at last. The Order of Frisbeetarians. We believe that when you die, your soul ascends to a rooftop and you can never get it back."

I like his uncertainty and his irreverence. I like mine, too. I wonder, though, about you. Do you have some sacred obligation to defend your way as the only way? I wonder. On the one hand, it must be very hard not to do that, given the history of the Vatican and the "one"

Holy Roman Catholic Church. On the other hand, you, Francis, don't seem to me like a *certainty* type of guy. God seems to be free of your need to control God. Or at least that is how I read you—and why I love you.

No Mention of God

What really gets to me is when people ask me not to mention God, whether in a marriage or a baptism or a funeral. I get phone messages that start with, "I have nothing against Jesus, but. . . ." A lot of people believe in God even though they can't stand to say the name. It makes them feel insincere to name a God they only slightly believe in. I understand.

I am a queer clergyperson, a renegade religionist. I live on the outskirts of religion in a small town called the Religious Left. From here, I quarrel with the punishmentalists in print, in the pulpit, and online. The punishmentalist theology can be summarized as "You're bad," and mine is summarized as "You're okay." We used to say, "I'm not okay, and you're not okay, and that's okay." That way we challenge the great binaries of heaven and hell, damned and saved, right and wrong, black and white, male and female. Now we have in my church, the UCC, new slogans, like "God Is Still Speaking," implying that whatever you heard God saying *then* is not what God might be saying *now*. With that slogan, we tried to render insignificant the seven or so passages in scripture that say gays are an abomination. We tried to take the concrete off ancient texts and give them a little air. Neither slogan—the okay one or the still-speaking one—got us on "Oprah," but at least we tried.

You probably don't know Thumbtack. It is a service for religious professionals that sends me about fifty requests a day from people who need a clergyperson to perform a wedding. The messages show up in your in-box, and you get to bid, naming the price of your service. The great majority of these requests contain this line: "No mention of God." This coded instruction is Exhibit A in why my Religious Left needs a new promotional campaign, or at least a chamber of commerce. It shows how successful the Religious Right has been in skewing religion to its most debased level. It also shows the extent of religion's moral injury. While trying way too hard to be right, religion has been on the wrong side of right. We queer and minority religious people lost God to the mean people.

True confession: my side lost. Our ideas about God not only receive no mention, but our antagonists have been so wrong about God that they've taken God into the unmentionables. My side doesn't believe much in winning and losing, so the offense is taken only at the commercial level. Even National Public Radio reports that "most Christians" are anti-gay, assuming that Christians only live on the wrongly right side of the road. Even those who might be our cultural friends don't know where we live or how to find us. That can't be completely their own fault. You and I contributed to this mess. We let God language become a weapon. We are both in a lot of trouble—we're losing membership, clout, and trust. It's our own fault. We didn't know how to stop our peers from besmirching the name of God with judgments far from the heart of Jesus.

NPR reporters aren't the only people oblivious to my small town. Say the word *clergy* at a cocktail party, and people start confessing their sins. "I so hope I haven't said something immoral, and I apologize for saying 'bullshit' to you." As if I were above bullshit, which I am not. We lost the branding campaign while the Right commercialized themselves as "Christian."

This letter is a confessional explanation of how we lost. We, too, are in the business of religion, the holy hatching, matching, and dispatching. I've been in that business for forty years, queering religion and quarreling with the Right's misrepresentation of it. We used to call this kind of letter *apologetics*. But I offer an unapologetic apology. I think you get the need to both apologize and not be apologetic about our need to apologize. I think you're also attempting a sophisticated apology for what people think religion is, which it is not.

When I celebrated my fortieth ordination anniversary last year, I was surrounded by my growing post-denominational-yet-Baptist-and-UCC congregation of queers, misfits, atheists, agnostics, Jews, and at least one lesbian Muslim and her child. I love our mixture and guard its open gates with all my heart. Even when we celebrate Communion, we're sure to say our table is open, so open that if you don't want to partake or feel insincere partaking, please don't partake. Some of my members require that point of view. They feel social pressure during our agape meal and refuse it. They don't want to do something insincere, especially around God. They'd rather do nothing than do something fake.

I tried to tell my pregnant Muslim member that at forty-nine, she was too old to single-parent. She lived in a five-flight walk-up and had a bad knee. She had the child, and I was wrong. I'm still okay, and she's still okay, and we're both okay, and I was wrong. She has a profound sense of God and is a beautiful mother. Is her God Jesus or Allah or some mixture? A mixture.

We often call ourselves the "perfect church for imperfect people" or the best church you can't find (imitating a bookstore in Montague, Massachusetts, that advertises "books you don't need in a place you can't find"). We are often wrong in my village of the Religious Left, even when discussing hatching or "planned" "parenthood." Still, people do need hatching, matching, and dispatching rituals, and we provide them. These rites of passage are the moments when people allow something like Spirit into their lives. You call the church a field hospital. I do, too. We are incredibly unsure about who God is in those hospitals. I know we have doctrines. I even respect doctrine. But it has very little to do with most of what I do every day. We can get over the "no mention of God," but then we have to say something honest about God, in public.

We do pretty well at the end of life, when the aperture is ever so slightly open to God. In the dispatching, we don't say, "Ashes to ashes, dust to dust." We say "Ashes to ashes, stardust to stardust." We love science. We love evolution. We like abortion, or at least its medical assist to maximum human agency. We think women are humans, not subhumans. We also think science and God are partners, if not lovers. We don't really believe in miracles. Instead, we think everything is a miracle. If we have a binary fight in us, it's the war between the desacralized and the sacralized. The Right has desacralized religion and turned it into a punishing and punishmentalist rulebook. Your religion suffers even more from this diminishment of the divine than we do. But I don't think you partake in that diminishment.

If it's not about kindness, it's not religion. Thus say the Sufis, and they're right. Kindness matters. Punishment, even feared punishment, hurts. You are kind, and that's bigger than a doctrine.

The religious wrong thinks religion is about sex, especially if women or gay people have it. Religion is sex-positive to us queers; sex is negative to those who drink their dualisms strong. I know you know that. I just wonder how you and I get our little truths out from under the weight of our awful histories.

We Repent One by One, Day by Day

When I did the memorial service for Gloria, a famous porn star—whose movies I don't think I ever saw, even though the packed house had—I assured them that Gloria was just becoming a new kind of star. Hell's fire is the projection of the punishmentalists. But it is not ours. We join the Chippewa in understanding that the stars are where we dance with our forebears in heaven. Carl Sagan thought so, too. These more environmentally friendly memorials could help us both praise the earth.

In my place on the outskirts, where we do not enjoy market share or megaphones, we queer and change religion quietly. We wonder if we should find a way to be more "well known" but really don't try, since we're so tolerant of alternative points of view. Will you be happy if Catholicism enjoys a return of members to its pews? Will I be happy if we fail less and are more successful? You know what we queers think: we have to fail at our larger complicities and succeed at failure, with the failed.

It embarrasses us to follow the Jesus who refuses to have an enemy and then go out and make enemies so that we can get the binary attention that the media enjoy. We know we could win more fights if we knew how to develop more enemies. Maybe we should have our testosterone level checked?

Tolerance is not necessarily a virtue, as it causes a lot of us to stay out of business that might actually be ours. Tolerance looks away too often. Thus gay teens commit suicide or war is permitted. We think "diversity" matters more than human life. You have to admire the religious wrong's passion about their point of view. Tolerance is our own version of sin, that great missing of the mark. Are you more tolerant or more passionate? I think you are more passionate and not that tolerant of tolerance. You mention God all the time, and I really like that about you.

We open the doors of the great merciful church, the real church, and one by one restore something like trust in something like God. We attend to Gloria and her friends. We do one wedding and one funeral and one baptism after another.

Weddings

One of my recent weddings was with a Hindu bride, also head of the New York City taxi drivers' association, and a Catholic groom, an Ecuadoran taxi driver. The Hindu service was one night, the Catholic service a second night, and our service the third. Our service was a blend. I wonder what you think about that: Does it scare you or amuse you, or both? I know it was a long premarital consultation. What else could we do but go long and go deep with each other?

Another wedding was with a Palestinian refugee and a Jewish princess—these are their words for themselves. Her parents were divorced twice, so she has a biological mother and father as well as two stepmothers and two stepfathers. His father is a nonobservant Muslim. Nevertheless, his father is requiring that she convert to Islam so as not to embarrass the family. She has agreed, then disagreed, then agreed; we all bow all the time to all sorts of things, don't we?

As we've struggled with the difficulty and hypocrisy of this requirement, we've had to ask the question of the First Commandment. The First Commandment for Jews and Christians is to love God above all. To what do we bow down if we are unbelievers or sort-of believers or Jews whose Jewish fathers have the biggest Christmas tree in Westchester? We bow down to the God-beyond-God or the center that is deeper than the well. The groom in this situation has told his father that he will also be converting to Judaism, if the requirement remains that she convert to Islam. An eye for an eye, and a tooth for a tooth! I wonder what you think about all this mixed-upness. I wonder if you judge it or are amused by it, as I am, or troubled by it, or what? I know you are with me and Bono, but how can you be pope and do that, too? (Not to mention divorce: What do you think about that? I am divorced from my first husband. I felt very sinful about it and also very glad we didn't go on making each other miserable.)

Another wedding took me by air to Miami then to Guatemala City, by van to Lake Atitlán, and by boat to Casa del Mundo, a boutique eco-hotel sketched into the mountains on the lake. The hotel shared its space with Mayan carvings in the rock walls. Frances, Chinese American and Catholic, was marrying Jacob, African American and Unitarian. Their parents were all still married, which is remarkable in and of itself—both sets of parents married forty-one years. This wedding planning started off like so many: "Let's leave God out of it." It ended in prayers and a ring-warming ceremony, where guests warmed the ring with prayers in their own words.

When I asked the couple why we had to go so far to get them married, at lakeside, at sunset, they said, "Because it was neither of our homes." They weren't sticking it to their parents so much as reaching for a new kind of home. I noted that they rarely sat with their parents during the ten meals we enjoyed in the hotel dining room. I wondered (as a parent myself of offspring their age) what the parents felt about that. In fact, now that I often marry my kids' peers at faraway places, I find myself strangely warmed by their unique independence and reach. I think we raised them to be globals and dare not be surprised when they turn out that way. I think you get global really well. You know that it is all one big ball. Don't we need a God that size, too?

A final example. It was the first lesbian wedding in Mexico to make the society page of *El País*. The mother of one of the brides got the article placed there. It had to do with interviewing all one hundred of the staff people for the three-day event about their attitudes toward gender and orientation. Then there were the silver sculptures in the great tree, the dance floor built over the swimming pool, and the sprinklers that were on automatic and sprayed all the guests at precisely 11 p.m. The wedding hit new highs in expense and new highs in imagination as well. There was a joy for three days that made the society page announcement look small. We knew we were doing something magnificently subversive. And some of us knew God was alive to it and in it.

We rebuild the church one by one. I know your priests are doing that. I wanted you to know I am doing it, too.

Unlike you, I am married. Happily. We end many of our conversations with "I love you" and have snuggles every morning that we're in the same bed, which is not every morning. We have known better, worse, richer, poorer, sickness, and health. We will continue to know them, together. I love the idea that you can be married to the same man three times. I have. I trust him more and more, not less and less, over time. I think what happens between his Jewishness and my Christianity is holy. I think you might even agree. Again, what do we do with the institutional lag besides follow our people one by one? How can we help them find God and mention God with joy?

Multifaith Motors On

Whether Tevye from *Fiddler on the Roof* likes it or not, 47 percent of marriages today are interfaith. Gay marriage was as rapid a social and cultural change as any of us can remember—unless you consider that my mother's best friend was a Catholic who married a Protestant and was widely shunned for marrying "outside" of the faith. In the twenty-first century, we will tip into what Diana Eck calls religious pluralism, the time when over 50 percent of us will marry outside our faith of origin. We won't just be diverse; we will also be plural. We will be different from each other. We may hold true to our faith of origin and find ourselves delightfully mixed up with others. Mestizo will be mundane, not queer. I certainly hope that won't ruin queers' reputation for abnormality, and that both of our churches will catch up with this fact and these percentages.

When it comes to hatching, matching, and dispatching, religious queers are hard at play in our small town on the outskirts of religion. We have surreptitious suspicions that intermarriage—by race, religion, and class, or all three—will save the world and stop wars, which are so often so deeply rooted in monocultures that don't and can't understand each other. We are also aware of the statistics about homogeneity. We understand Tevye's fear about his future. We also know that he is misguided—that miscegenation and mixture and mess are all part of our road to unconditionality. We're also fully tempted by the conceit implied in this embrace of the mixed rather than the pure. We have a tendency to put down the purists, if not going all the way to demonizing them.

Someone rightly said that ageism is fear of our future self. Tevya's fear is not just about his grandchildren. It's also fear of his future self and the culture that will surround his future self. It will be *different*.

We offer Tevye that uncanny hope of connected life, instead of being buried in the Jewish part of the cemetery. We even imagine that the environment will be resacralized by dethroning the human from our disappointing and dangerous throne. Queer religionists most of all want out of the double binds of the dualisms: girl/boy, good/bad, right/wrong, pure/mixed, secular/religious, Catholic/Protestant. We want a new synthesis that is large enough to hold us and God together.

When it comes to the hatching, we want to assure that the child comes into a village and not just a couple. We want the child to be dedicated to more perfect parents than the child's parents can possibly be. When it comes to the dispatching, we refer to the stars, not the dust. When it comes to hatching, matching, and dispatching, we don't mind not mentioning God so much as we mind being told not to mention God. We acknowledge the tremendous harm God language and God belief and God quarrels cause. We acknowledge. We see. We understand. And we wonder what will happen to unconditional love if the energy behind the yearning for God can't be mentioned. We don't like it when people say, "Baptize my baby, and don't mention God." We take that opportunity to say something good about God. I think you and I agree here. How can we redeem God language, which is even more important than connecting the environment and the economy

to God? How can God be praised in our words and
actions? That's the important thing.

Aiming at Authority

Authority, according to your newly popular Roman
Catholic Church, has four sources: natural law, reason,
experience, and scriptural theology. You could write
the whole history of the Christian Church by its distor-
tions of these four items. You could even say we rebal-
ance these every century or so. In Protestantism right
now, we're rebalancing toward experience, particularly
as feminists and queers have blown the theological
house down with a heightened emphasis on the Holy
Spirit. Natural law and reason had their days during the
Enlightenment, when the only thing we were taught
to do in seminary is apply critical thinking to ancient
texts. Theology had its heyday much earlier, when
Aquinas and Aristotle had their system of thesis, antith-
esis, and synthesis to solve Trinitarian squabbles. I am
thinking you are in a grand rebalancing of the Roman
Catholic understanding of authority, kind of moving in
my direction. Maybe that is just my projection?

Sociologists often argue that authority is the ability to control oneself. I like to apply experiential,

Third-Person-of-the-Trinity theology to that great insight about human maturity. I like to say that authority is not just about control of self or management of self or manipulation of self or even realization of self, it is about *aiming* the self. We aim toward the bull's-eye, and even when we're good at it, we hit it every now and then. Never forget that a great baseball hitter has an average of .300 or so. That means great hitters don't hit the ball two out of three times at bat.

Authority is the ability to aim. Authority is the ability not to aim or control others but to aim yourself. I like where you are aiming yourself, Francis: to the world, not the church. That's a funny thing for a pope to do, but not a funny thing for a new kind of pope to do. You're our first interfaith pope. Or multifaith pope. You haven't left behind Jesus so much as his falsely propped-up authority.

A lot of words have been polluted, and *authority* surely joins their team. Authority is frequently abused. At the moment, we are all but destroying the erotic power, our enthusiasms, by boundary-training sessions. In my church, which has a lot less trouble with pedophilia than yours, we are required to take these boundary-training classes, which translated by the insurance companies means, "Don't sleep with your

congregants." Ever. I'm not going to make a long complaint about boundary training, because I know it's good
and necessary and right, given the horror of abuse. But I
will say that it can also destroy the bodily spirits and erotic
powers of clergy with authority. We have to be careful not
to throw the baby out with the baptismal water.

Or if you don't want to talk about sex any more,
let's talk about the oft-cited complaint about clergy:
that we have "control problems." I daresay it's a common diagnosis of leadership today, and not just in the
church. Many corporate executives are said to have the
same problem, trying to control what they can't. You
seem to have avoided that trap. I don't get the sense
that you're trying to control much. But you are inviting
many to many versions of personal authority.

Clergy need to worry more about our authority
than our boundaries. Why? Because rightly by natural
law, we are granted democratic authority with others.
They actually listen to our sermons every week—the
very ones who sign our paychecks and bother us when-
ever they get a chance. I find that amazing. Natural law
is the source of leadership. It is natural and democratic
to govern ourselves by consensual principles.

Clergy need to critique authority with reason. Reason is good. Thinking is good. Critical thinking is even

better. You don't have to throw out the whole Enlightenment because it became stale bread. The only thing wrong with critical thinking is that people sometimes overdo it and can't also experience things or be a part of a democratic group or be empathic about the humility of theologizing, as in thinking about God.

You and I probably disagree greatly about governance and about papal authority. I would love to know what you really think it is, coming from the global south to the northern Vatican. What I see is that you are thinking a new thought about authority and control and boundaries, and I want to know more.

Our authority comes from our love of reason and natural law. It also comes from scriptural theology. People ask me if I know God well enough to help them find God. They ask if I understand scripture well enough to crack it open. People ask if I know God well enough to help them find God. You are helping millions return to the place where they might be willing to mention God. Wow.

As you have shown us so well, the ministry is putting together these four distortable paths to authority in a way that gives them authenticity. It's in the thread of the grail that authority is found. It is something like that great underground river of death-dealing and life-giving blood. It's something we know is there yet can never really see. And this explanation could be brought higher. It is what Dan Brown meant and what thrilled all his readers in the *Da Vinci Code*. The Grail is the female version of Jesus, underground, tying things together, but not visibly so. In knowing the threads of the Grail, we know what you call ecological integrity.

Do we hold together? Are we also people who experience the divine, or do we distort the divine? Are we respectful enough of other people's paths to God to allow them to respect ours? What a difference that would make the next time we go to ground zero together to bury our dead, the ones who died because we couldn't respect each other's religions.

I am thinking ministry is walking these four paths to authority simultaneously. We reason our way to God. We self-govern our way to God. We theologize our way to God. And we experience God. No, this is not a TED Talk but a thread talk, one honoring the Holy Grail that connects all these paths to each other. When we let ourselves be ordained by people, and by the Holy Spirit, we grail ourselves. We thread ourselves. We put ourselves together.

We aim ourselves. Authority is the ability to aim, not the ability to hit every target all the time. Welcome to the one holy Catholic and apostolic church. It misses a lot and will continue to miss a lot. But we can still aim. We can still thread the air, fire, water, and earth of the four pathways and experience God in the aiming and the threading. For fun, try to match air, fire, water, and earth to reason, natural law, theology, and experience. What we really mean by the priesthood of all believers is here. We are all theologians, threading our way to multiple meanings.

Ravi, my colleague who runs the New Sanctuary Movement out of our church's building, told me a story about preaching when in prison because he was undocumented. He wasn't ordained. He hadn't been to seminary. He did experience the Spirit. The guards started coming to his services. When he left jail, they gave him a Bible. But he didn't get to take it with him. It went missing. Don't you hope somebody stole it so that they could be the next jail preacher? I do. A lot of us have lost our Bibles. Ravi is still undocumented and also leads people to accompany two hundred other undocumented people a week to their weekly Immigration and Customs Enforcement check-ins. Before I get too concerned about your religious authority, or mine, make sure I introduce you to Ravi.

Jesus said, "All power is given unto me in heaven and in earth" (Matthew 28:18 KJV). We aim toward Jesus. An old hymn says, "This is my story, this is my song." Jesus is the grail and thread of our story and our song. We aim toward Jesus. You and I are friends because of our aim toward him. We are also friends with Bono because of Bono's aim for him. Bono loses his Frisbee on the roof; we, like Ravi, lose our Bibles, too. Our authority is in our aim, not in our being right about God.

Love,
Donna

7

Dear Francis, Hemming and Hawing

Dear Francis,

I will never touch you the way you have touched me.
You made a big turn in my life, and I will be always be
a part of your fan base. That is all, and that is (maybe)
enough for me. You have been a major spiritual antidepressant for me. Thank you, thank you, and thank you.

I promise to stop writing you for a while after
this letter. For now, let me say good-bye, the kind of
good-bye that always has a hello in it, the same way

every death contains a resurrection and every curse a blessing. How does that work? You know. It works the way the earth works, constantly changing, closing one window to open another door, dealing enough with our grief that we find our way to "My Lord, What a Morning." Your work has been such a blessing to so many—and it has almost taken away from the many curses your institution has also made. My institution is the same: we have bored people on their way to God—that is, when we weren't judging them. The massive transition we are always making back to the throne of a gracious God will remain incomplete. You and I both know that. But we will still try and try and try again.

I've had three major love themes in my letters to you. One is the way we both love justice and hate that it does not prevail. The other is the way we both love the earth and its animals and its waters and hate that the great bio of diversity does not prevail. That is what you name so well as ecological integrity. The way all the parts make the whole, from the smaller to the larger, even the smallest to the largest. We love the earth the same way—politically, fiercely, from its bottom to its top, its valleys to its mountains. We try to love the way Jesus tried to love, which includes loving our enemies, even refusing to have an enemy of any created thing or soul. And, of course, we fail.

We have also had our quarrels, each of which is embedded in the way we love. We have that pesky hem business and that pesky fence business and that pesky gender issue. I keep thinking women and GLBTQ people are part of the whole—and you do, too. But your institution does not. We need to keep fussing over this until we either get it right or don't get it right and decide that we won't be able to. I love you too much to stop hoping your magnificent sense of ecological integrity will integrate all of us ecos, back to the time before the snake and the apple and their tricks.

The Way You Love Animals

Of course, you did not write the *Laudato Si'* encyclical as a love letter to me. I just read it that way. "We are not God. The earth was here before us and was given to us," you wrote. "We are not faced with two separate crises, one environmental and the other social, but rather one complex crisis which is both social and environmental." I read these words and respect your power to say them and am thrilled that somebody got a best seller out of the obvious. You named the encyclical after Saint

Francis of Assisi's *Canticle of the Sun*, in which the early Francis praises God for animals and creation. I won't go on too long about my dog and my cat and my love for them, but you should know that I love nature and animals as much as you do.

In a recent record-breaking snowstorm in New York City, where two feet fell in twelve hours, burying cars completely and people partially, I learned a lot about what matters to me. My dog getting a proper walk matters to me. My cat's litter box cleaned out matters a lot to me. I have always loved the way my husband fills the bird feeders, and when it snows, I love his habitual care of things that fly even more delightful.

Filling the bird feeders is practically a spiritual practice for him. He likes the way the birds fly into our tiny patch of yard, and so do I. They make the concrete jungle of our abode more appealing. We were also slightly short of groceries the day of the big snow and totally out of chocolate, our usual dessert after a meal (we can usually make a good bar last a week, and when you eat a lot of garlic, it's always nice to have the countertaste of sweet at the end of a meal). Thus, my lament as a well-fed first-worlder that night of the big snow was this: "I wish I had something sweet to eat." It wasn't a real complaint, just an overall wistfulness, laden with appreciation for my normal days and their normal ways.

Warren went out and scooped up some of the clean snow and poured maple syrup on it. It was delicious. He wasn't filling up the bird feeders but could have been. Our dessert was sweet and good, cheap and available, making a delight amidst a storm. I don't want to put Ben and Jerry's out of business, even in the winter, but suffice it to say that their new flavor, Swirl, brought out for the Paris climate talks, is almost as good as syrup on snow.

I would like to tell you that my dog is a low-cost form of personal entertainment, like syrup on snow. But that would belie how much our lovely vet charges to keep her in a licensed collar or fit to attend a kennel from time to time. I'd like to tell you that our cat was a low-cost form of personal entertainment too, but she often nudges me when I am on the computer, turning me into a raving maniac because when I want to type, I want to type. I am a fully nonrepentant buyer of the proposed Anthropocene Epoch.

What matters to me is being able to love my dog, my cat, my husband, and all sweet things, not necessarily in that order.

I also love the way you praise animals. You get them. You would like my cat, Hudson, long deceased, buried outside my window, who was my best friend for years. You would love my current upstate cat, Dutchess, named for the county where we sometimes live, and my current downstate cat, Gracie, a real bruiser of a beast. Cats, says the T-shirt, exist to show us that not everything has a purpose. When you speak of animals and nature, you get rid of their purpose, their instrumentality, the way they are supposed to serve us. You say the purpose is to praise, and that's where I sing with you the most. I am so tired of fixing things or thinking my life is a fix-it shop or myself a repairperson.

You would also like my relatively new dog, who is in heat right now, bleeding a tad on the floor. Sybil is her name. She is named after a famous Hudson Valley revolutionary, Sybil Luddington, who rode a bit longer than Paul Revere on the same mission. I won't bring up our chickens, or the goats we raised when our kids were little, or even the goat that my sons birthed at ages six and eight, when my husband and I were out for the evening and the teenagers next door were in charge. The children used the *New York Times* blue plastic wrapping to cover their hands and help the goat, named after Angie of the Grimke sisters. Like you and me and the cats, the boys were useless. Angie didn't mind the companionship. The babysitters fled, and I still love them.

On a recent California vacation, we enjoyed many lovable things, including friends, food, and wine. But what we will remember are the animal moments. First we saw a coyote. I'd never seen one before. Then we watched a mother cow play with her calf, nudging her away affectionately, so much so that I had to declare myself anthropomorphizing. Then we stayed at River's End in Jenner, California, where the sea lions gather to take in the morning sun after their morning swim and frolic. (I hope you find time to frolic somehow. I really do.)

There is more to love than we could possibly love. We can't survive without the chance to love stuff and souls other than our own. But with that love, we can more than survive. We can even find our way to enchantment and what you so rightly call praise.

In the encyclical, you remind us, "We read in the Gospel that Jesus says of the birds of the air that 'not one of them is forgotten before God' (*Luke* 12:6). How then can we possibly mistreat them or cause them harm?" You also call on us all to be better stewards of all creation, noting, "Each organism, as a creature of God, is good and admirable in itself." You condemn the

view that humankind has "absolute domination over
other creatures" as a misinterpretation of God's grant
of "dominion" over creation. You say, "Our indiffer-
ence or cruelty toward fellow creatures of this world
sooner or later affects the treatment we mete out to
other human beings. We have only one heart, and the
same wretchedness, which leads us to mistreat an animal, will not be long in showing itself in our relation-
ships with other people." Every act of cruelty toward
any creature is against human dignity. You also directly
address animal testing, noting, "The *Catechism of the Catholic Church* teaches that experimentation on animals is
morally acceptable only if it remains within reasonable
limits [and] contributes to caring for or saving human
lives. . . . Human power has limits and . . . it is contrary
to human dignity to cause animals to suffer or die need-
lessly." Amen. Some people wonder if this is really the
kind of thing that a pope should talk about. I say the
opposite: what kind of pope would *not* talk about matters animal in nature? Why be a religious leader at all
if you don't talk about real things for real people and
real animals? Why be a religious leader and not bother
people? You bother us by jumping the fence built to
keep the power of popes—and religion—from holding
sway. Creation is in your debt.

The Way You Love Justice

You say, "We need to reject a magical conception of the market, which would suggest that the problems can be solved simply by an increase in the profits of companies or individuals." I am so tired of being trickled down upon. Capitalism has worked only if its objective was to consolidate wealth in the 1 percent or, as a new study shows, in the hands of sixty-one people who have more than half of the wealth of the world. That kind of concentration of power and wealth is just plain wrong. It offends God's intention in creation. We both know it—and you have aimed your power to bust up the concentration. You don't need to know how being poor hurt me and my father and my mother and my sister and my brother. We are the least of the problem—and we got out. But the ongoing nature of injustice breaks my heart. I don't care how lucky I am or will be. I won't forget the humiliation and degradation of early poverty. I think you know what I mean.

History shows us that without protections, an unrestrained market will ignore and even reward the violent marginalization of inconvenient populations, both human and nonhuman. You see how this is especially true when market forces are married to the imperative to

use technology to do things cheaper and faster, regard-
less of moral cost. You call us to resist an amoral rush
to consume via technology in an unrestrained market.
This disconnects us not only from the proper value of
the things we consume and of the people who work to
bring those goods to us, but ultimately from ourselves.
Consumerism is a soul-crushing practice, designed spe-
cifically to leave us unsatisfied so we keep on consum-
ing more and more with no end in sight. While this
might benefit the stock prices of big corporations, it
kills the human spirit—and, significantly, the wider
creation. As you argue in the encyclical, the ecological
crisis is primarily a spiritual crisis. We not only need
new laws, we need to become different kinds of people,
living our lives in fundamentally different ways.

You want a new kind of asceticism, one that cul-
tivates new practices of resistance to "greed and com-
pulsion" and instead sees creation as something more
than merely a set of objects to be "used and con-
trolled." That's why I only buy clothes and furniture
in thrift shops. That's why I uselessly raise chickens or
goats. I like the way they look and the eggs and milk
they make. I could get those products much cheaper
at Walmart, but I don't think they are products in the
first place.

I like the renewable, and I hate stores that are shiny and expensive. I love the way you challenge capitalism spiritually in such a way as to allow spiritual strength to political and scientific responses. What has been missing from community organization and public policy is spiritual oomph. You give it to us. Thank you again.

The Way You Love Water

In Psalm 93:4, God is referred to as "mightier than the breakers of the sea." The psalmist is writing a press release for Almighty God, whose capacity is mightier than the breakers of the sea. You describe water as a "basic and universal human right." Therefore, Nestlé should stop buying up streams so it can do to water what it tried to do to breast milk. They want to sell water, just like they wanted to sell breast milk.

I should stop carrying a water bottle that advertises my obedience to a culture of portability, so interested in its short term that it is willing to industrialize the oceans and dehydrate the poor. You probably agree with me. Water is not a commodity. God's power is as mighty as the roll of the sea. You probably join me in not knowing how to swim in this ocean of utter power and utter impotence shaking hands in a water bottle or a corporation's mind. The word *should* about the water bottle comes to mind. At least I use ones that are recycled.

Jeffrey Hollender, the entrepreneur who provided the funding for Seventh Generation, which makes eco-friendly household and personal-care products, says the route to a freely hydrated world is in "radical transparency." By that, he means talking about what it's like to sell expensive toilet paper and detergent that doesn't work as well as the toxic kind. Hollender named the price and the difficulty of de-polluting. He led a company whose products were more expensive than other products—and he succeeded in getting people to buy them. He learned how to unlearn. He helped people unlearn. He re-worlded the commerce of paper products and insisted that people understand that doing good is better than doing less bad. He showed us that it will cost us. Now many people want higher taxes to pay for more beautiful and less toxic infrastructure. People pay more for vegetables that are organically grown. People are not stupid. We know how the Nestlés of the world are commodifying things that cannot and should not be commodified. We also don't know yet how to live without money or oil. You are helping us find our way.

How do you make a case for God's breakers in a world that is trying to break you? You name the difficulty. You embrace the difficulty. You might even love the difficulty. You know we need to fall and fail on our way to ecological integrity. We are far off the created path. We are way off, and we are lost. You are shepherding us back.

You remember what a famous drunk said: "I don't drink much, but that other person, not I, when she drinks, drinks a lot." You help us become the kind of people we hope to be and want to be. With the kind of spiritual power for forgiveness and self-love that we find in our beloved traditions, we have the power to break the breakers that are breaking us and to go with the glow and flow of God. We both believe that. That's why we are such good friends.

I Love the Way You Put It All Together

You base ecological integrity in a theological idea—taught by John Paul II and Benedict XVI as well—that all creation has intrinsic value. You argue that ecological wholeness and beauty, as well as justice and fairness, are the way that things are meant to be from the beginning. We are created for goodness, not for plenty for a few and violence against the many. The way things are now is out of sync with our creation. No wonder so many of us are so miserable. We are out of the way. We are off the path. We are not who we are meant to be.

You, however, have presented so many ideas so well and so comprehensively in your encyclical:

> "It is not enough, however, to think of different species merely as potential 'resources' to be exploited, while overlooking the fact that they have value in themselves" (par. 33).

> "Where certain species are destroyed or seriously harmed, the values involved are incalculable" (par. 36).

> "We must forcefully reject the notion that our being created in God's image and given dominion over the earth justifies absolute domination over other creatures" (par. 67).

> Creation has "an intrinsic value," which is "independent of [its] usefulness. Each organism, as a creature of God, is good and admirable in itself" (par. 140).

You want us to think about the interrelated ecology of the human and nonhuman. You want us to think about the interrelated ecology of many different kinds of humans and many different kinds of humans. Integral ecology explicitly "takes us to the heart of what it is be human" (par. 11). With these ideas, you have started a new reformation, a new regeneration, a new way to return us all and each to our roots in creation. Isn't it funny that all this is happening in the five hundredth anniversary of the Protestant Reformation, when my people successfully broke away from your people? I guess we're having a reunion.

Just about everything has a life cycle; just about nothing doesn't have a life cycle. The circumstances of the Reformation's birth have disappeared. We are no longer awed at the printing press, or early industrial-ization, or an urgency to read our own Bible. We are astonished at dead factories and repurposing them in just about every town and city that has one. We read our own Bible, almost in a lonely way, so successful was the individualization released by the Reformation. We don't even know where a printing press is but will look it up on Google as soon as we get a chance.

I love the way you enter the moment. In your hom-ily at Lampedusa, on July 8, 2013, you said,

> Immigrants dying at sea, in boats which were vehi-cles of hope and became vehicles of death. When I

first heard of this tragedy a few weeks ago, and realized that it happens all too frequently, it has constantly come back to me like a painful thorn in my heart. So I felt that I had to come here today, to pray and to offer a sign of my closeness, but also to challenge our consciences lest this tragedy be repeated. Please, let it not be repeated!

As you did at ground zero, you entered the cave of death. You showed up. You didn't act as if you didn't see what was going on. I wonder how you hold yourself together. I know your ideas hold together. They hold together beautifully. But what about you?

I can imagine there are many days when you'd rather not show up but instead cave in. In *The Flight of Monsieur Monde*, the French writer Georges Simenon tells of a man who headed out for the office and but walked on by. He left for a long time and eventually just returned to the office. Maybe you'd like to do the same. How do you rest when boats of life become boats of death? How do you pray? How do you stay sane?

I hope you take time off. Everybody thinks you are going to pull Catholicism to the global south, so introduce some healthy customs from there. Afternoons are for a siesta, a caesura, a pause, a rest. I wonder if you are rich in rest, not just obsessed with the poor. I know you identify with the poor. You say, "I dream of the church that is of the poor and for the poor." In what ways are you poor? I know you refused the big, fancy apartment. I like that about you.

I also like how you really care about the stuff you care about and don't care about what little traps people lay for you. When someone said to you that condoms have holes, instead of being shocked by someone bringing up a sexual matter in front of your highness and your holiness, you said that condoms can't be useful if they have holes. In that casual retwist, you really did something different: you turned a weird story into a weirder story, and everyone loved it. You don't like the press or play the game of playing to them, and you don't give them much time. Is that why they like you so much?

Your small deeds and your large deeds coalesce into a different kind of ecological integrity, one where gestures matters as much as deeds and encyclicals. I am glad you don't have an e-mail account. I like that about you. I'm thinking the Roman curia has already lost control of you. And then I'm wondering what you will do with your freedom, in addition to making sure you get enough rest. I am now going to bother you again and then say good-bye, but please know that my bothering you has to do with how much I love you. You put so much together so well. Why not a little more?

That Pesky Hem and That Pesky Closed Table

Here I want to underthink the matter of touch and just touch it. The kind of touch I intend is the kind when someone just grazes your arm when she sees you are on the verge of tears. Francis, may I? May I touch you with words? We have only been in the same time and space and time zone twice. Both times matter. While others struggled to touch you, I refrained from such contact. In my benediction to you here, I will use words to tell you why.

Touch is just a slight connection, one that doesn't invade and doesn't intrude so much as it simply connects. When the touch is over, it's over. It doesn't do anything, like change the world or change the motion of the world or assuage heartbreak. Instead it touches. Touch touches. We are touched by touch. Enough already. Sometimes I just get really sick of words. In the name of underthinking touch, I am already overthinking it. Even scriptural study can take you too far into the weeds.

You remember that story I was writing about earlier? The one about the woman who touched Jesus' hem? Luke records, "She came up behind him and touched the edge of his cloak" (8:44 NIV); the word translated "edge" is Greek *kraspedon*, referring to the edge, border, or hem of a garment. But it can also refer to the "tassel" that Israelites wore on the four corners of the cloak. Whatever a hem is on a tunic, I don't know. I do know that the woman in Luke's account had to go down to go up, that she had to choose to acknowledge Jesus' power and then was healed. But what about her power? I don't want to pick a fight with Jesus. You know, I hope, that I love him. What I love less is the way we dive into the weeds about Jesus instead of touching him. You touch him. I like that.

It reminds me of everything I know about leadership. If the leader is constantly getting bigger and the people are constantly getting smaller, that is not leadership. That is followership, not leadership.

There are surely two kinds of New Yorkers—the kind who see Meryl Streep on the street and rush to get her photograph and the kind who see Meryl Streep on the street and quietly look at her. I am the latter kind. The paparazzi approach to fame just plain bugs me. So I'm set up not to like Jesus' approach to the hemorrhaging woman and frankly not to be that crazy about her approach to him either. I surely respect my friend's difference.

I can't help but think that famous people, including you and Jesus and Meryl Streep, are like ordinary people. I don't think you are anything different or that ordinary people should debase ourselves on our way to knowing your power. I even think that knowing your power should mean we know our own power better.

Seriously, consider the Oscars. All those famous, important, rich people can't find a black actor or actress to honor? They are behaving in a most ordinary way.

You told us in Philadelphia to go down the hall and touch the hem of the woman whom no one touches. You spoke about the internal and external assaults on the family, a point of view I mightily appreciate. You get that people are oppressed in their capacity to take care of their own children, often having to take care of others in order to take care of their own. You understand what the Republicans love to call personal responsibility. You believe we have more spiritual power than we think we do. You don't think we are fully oppressed— and you understand how we often participate in our own oppression.

We are to be the Jesus touch to each other. We are not to debase ourselves for him and touch his hem, his edge, and his outer parts. We are to touch each other. By the way, my main struggle with the way I appreciate you is here. I don't want you to be that effective. I want your tap on our shoulder to become the beginning of a great democratic movement, one in which we stand side by side, not up or down to each other. I don't want Naomi Klein to be that big a leader either. I want a movement that grows us up each and all, gives us a role, brings us to full democratic maturity. I think you want that as well. I think you are actually smart enough and humble enough to know about up and down, in and out, and about leadership.

Part of the way institutions—and gods—scare us is by our consent to believe that they have more power than they really do. Please don't get too puffed up. Act with authority, which means act and speak without forcing consent.

When leaders do too much, they lose the abilities of their followers to follow. The best leaders create leaders around them. They open one table after another to the people who thought they'd never be invited anywhere.

You cannot save the planet alone, nor would a spiritual grown-up want you to do so. You also can't ordain women, help immigrants, punish predator priests, challenge capitalism, and restore humility to Rome, even if you stay longer than the five years you have promised. You can and should point toward these things. You can lead by setting direction and even issue an edict or two. But, as you are doing with *Laudato Si'*, better to persuade us and teach us and talk to us than to boss us around. We need to hear that you want women's ordination and GLBTQ people's ordination and open tables—and that you want us to figure out how to make these things happen. Lasting change comes with consent. Reactivity sets in when leaders go too fast or refrain from bringing their constituents along with them. Bring us along.

Act. Just act. Don't enforce consequences. Show us the way to each other's hems and each other's power. Direct us to the ordination of women and gays and to full communion at open tables. Move us from spiritual adolescence to spiritual maturity. Trust us to be healed and to rise and to touch each other's hems. And then take a well-deserved nap.

———

As I've been finishing this last letter, another friendship has been revealed, an intimate friendship that developed between Pope John Paul II and a philosopher, Anna-Teresa Tymieniecka. They were good friends for three decades, and of course everyone assumed the relationship was sexually intimate when it was apparently just intimate. I'll admit to being a bit envious of their friendship.

I said at the beginning of this letter that I was possibly satisfied with being a follower of your leadership. The truth is, I would like more. Maybe we could go camping together? Or find a way to share articles that intrigue us? Or do more Bible study?

You know I'm a happily married woman. I love the man who fills up the bird feeders and brings in snow for syrup. I also don't really need any more friends. Once I made a vow to absolutely not have any other friends because I wasn't taking good enough care of the ones I had. That day I met a Jewish woman who writes extraordinary liturgy. She calls it "liturgy without God." We became friends. I got the message: I was not to close down but instead agree to be opened up.

If I were bold enough to ask for a friendship with you, how would I do it? I would say that when both of our works are done, when you have taken all the risks you can and I have done the same, how about we become friends and learn to rest and praise and talk together? Camping? Looking at the different colors of moss and praising God for being so effusive and extravagant? Petting a cat? Doing nothing? Napping in the sunny corners of our queer-friendly assisted-living facility? Singing together, especially the last verse? You've done so much for earth. Heaven owes you!

Lots of people think they are going to meet you when they cross the pearly gates. I so wish I could meet you before then.

Love,
Donna